First published in the United Kingdom in 2008 by
Pavilion Books
Old West London Magistrates Court
10 Southcombe Street
London, W14 0RA

An imprint of Anova Books Company Ltd

Design and layout © Pavilion, 2008
Text © Kate Shirazi, 2008
Photography © Pavilion, 2008, except images on pages 4, 6, 13, 36, 41, 52, 64
which are courtesy of cakeadoodledo.co.uk

Commissioning editor: Emily Preece-Morrison
Designer: Lotte Oldfield
Home economist and stylist: Kate Shirazi
Photography: Charlotte Barton
Copy editor: Siobhan O'Connor
Indexer: Patricia Hymans

ISBN 978-1-862058-10-1

A CIP catalogue record for this book is available from the British Library.

10 9 8

Reproduction by Rival Colour, United Kingdom
Printed and bound by Toppan Leefung Printing Ltd, China

www.anovabooks.com

# Contents

# Introduction

There has been intensive research carried
out on the healing power of cake...

Scientists, nutritionists and psychiatrists have all spent hours pondering the curative qualities of the cupcake (possibly). Can cupcakes be classed as a "health food"? Probably not, but they cheer you up and make you smile. So that's good enough for me.

Bought cakes that come in boxes and sit on supermarket shelves hold fond memories of a childhood Saturday afternoon treat. We (three children) would pester Mum, and sometimes she would give in and a cake would be bought. When we got home, the family of five would stare at this *small* round foamy sponge with a red, red jam and whiter-than-white "cream" filling. Yumm-eeeee. The cake would be sliced with surgical precision by the appointed "cutter". It had to be fair. Each slice would be examined at length by me, my brother and my sister, in order to determine whether one slice was bigger and therefore "unfair". The you-cut-I-choose rule was enforced with a rod of iron. Once the cutter had performed their task, they had to stand back and wait for the agonizing choice by the siblings. This extended doling-out of the small cake to the greedy family simply served to add to the deliciousness of it all. Looking at one of those cakes now, I wonder how we managed to get five slices out of it.

This is where the cupcake has so many things going for it. There's the element of built-in portion control. Fairness without the fuss. But how *many* should be eaten? Arguments may arise – and there must be room for an argument somewhere. My answer would be: eat

ten in one go and you are a pig and deserve to get fat. One mate ate five with no bother at all, and left the table clutching another one "for later". My five-year-old can easily pack away two, but as a responsible mother I then stop him before he stuffs another three into his face (and he would, too ...). The jury is out here. My feeling is that two is acceptable, but I know others who hold different views ...

Cake is a luxury and a treat, but that doesn't mean that baking has to be difficult, complicated or make you sweaty with anxiety. Cupcakes are particularly easy to produce. This is not me being all cocky because I make them all day, every day. I am a firm believer in the process being as enjoyable as the result. They really are easy. What is truly gratifying is that, when you present a plate of cupcakes to your admiring audience, they will gasp and smile and tell you how clever you are – and will secretly be cursing you for your aesthetic culinary skills. Let them inwardly worry about their own cupcake shortfalls. Wallow in the smugness. Just don't let them know that they took five minutes to knock up and three to decorate. You see – cupcakes are good for you in a truly holistic way. You don't even need to eat the darlings to make yourself feel better.

Kate

www.cakeadoodledo.co.uk

# Ingredients and equipment

Top tips for getting yourself kitted out and stocked up.

If you are reading this, it is more than likely that you have a roof over your head and the ability to make a few choices about what you do and don't want to eat. Lucky you and lucky me, quite frankly. This isn't meant to be a lecture, but I do like the idea of making a cake with a conscience. If you are going be bothered to make a cake, make it with nice ingredients. I am not saying that everything has to be organic and grown within a 150-foot radius of your dwelling, but why not use good-quality cocoa (Green & Black's organic cocoa does make the best chocolate cake *ever*) or unwaxed lemons (who wants to eat a load of wax?). And please, please, *please*, use free-range eggs. If you'd seen my hens the day they had been rescued from the battery, you'd use free-range eggs, too. Phew. I think I'll just go and lie down on my organic fair-trade lavender-scented hemp mattress and chew on some fennel seeds ...

Now on to some other ingredients' top tips. Strike me down and write an apoplectic letter to the newspaper if it makes you happy, but I really think cakes are better made with soft margarine rather than butter. There. I've said it. The world continues to turn and I do believe that the roof hasn't been struck by lightning. Most things are better with butter: pastry, cheese sauce, scones ... and I wouldn't want margarine melting onto my crumpet, thank you very much. I just feel that you get a more consistently light sponge with a soft margarine. It's up to you entirely and you'll see recipes for both, but using a soft margarine means that you can bung all the ingredients into one bowl and whizz away. It can't get any easier.

You will see that I am partial to a drop of colour on my cake. I remember one woman wanting reassurance that the electric-blue cake that little Crispin was about to tuck into was entirely natural. I looked at the vivid blue and looked at her and had to break it to her that, in fact, there was nothing very natural about a food item that bright. Having said that, there are companies out there (Sugarflair for instance - available widely) who produce quite a range of tartrazine-free colours for those whose eyes start spinning and their skin forming a thin film of sweat when it comes to artificial colours – and that's just the parents waiting for their children to absorb the colour and go on a behaviour free fall. But think of the possibilities of harnessing the energy from a small child in the throes of a colour-induced frenzy of hyperactivity. I may have just solved one of the biggest eco-conundrums of our time. You see? Cupcakes! I tell you.

Back to colour, gels are much better than the liquid colourings. They don't thin the icing and the colours tend to be much more versatile. I love them. You can get them from good kitchen shops and sugarcraft specialists. Word of warning: a little goes a long way.

# Encasing your cupcakes

Just to make things ever so slightly complicated, cupcake cases (baking cups) come in different sizes. Don't worry. As long as you use a deep 12-hole muffin tin (pan) to put the cases in, it really doesn't matter whether you choose to use the standard readily available case, a muffin case or a middling-size case. I use the middle size, which are usually American, by Wilton, and called "standard party cups". They are sold in lots of kitchen and sugarcraft shops, and can easily be bought on-line. But really, go for what you want or can get your hands on. Stands to reason that if you are using a smaller case, you'll get a few more cakes and the cooking time may be shorter, and vice versa for muffin cases. The only really important thing is to place the cases in a muffin tray before you put the mixture in. So please take my blithe comments about how many cakes are produced by every recipe as a guide only. Don't take the cooking times to heart, either. They are also a guide. All ovens cook differently, and I don't want to be responsible for your burnt or raw cakes. Cakes are done if they are firm to the touch and a bit springy on top. You can also insert a cocktail stick (toothpick) into the centre – if it comes out clean, the cake is done. Blackened charcoal, not good. Neither is your finger disappearing into the centre goo of the cake as you prod.

# Wheat and gluten

Unfortunately, some people seem to inflate at a rate of knots at the merest hint of gluten. In fact, just the word spoken out loud is enough to send some people scuttling. There are, of course, several conditions such as coeliac and Crohn's disease where gluten and particularly wheat are not a good idea, and certainly not something to be made fun of. Does this mean no cake? No, sirree. Please refer to "healing power of cake" as mentioned before. You can get gluten-free flour and I have been known to rustle up the odd ("odd" being the operative word) creation. Having had several interesting and not altogether successful baking sessions, I decided to throw caution to the wind and dispense with flour altogether. Ground almonds. They are the way forward. You get a delicious sponge with none of the "What's this weird cake made out of?" element. Just a glorious moist and utterly delicious cake. See recipes on p.46, p.50 and p.105.

# Piping bags

If you choose to undertake some piping, and I hope you do, may I make a suggestion? Buy a packet of parchment piping (decorating) bags. They are small, one-use wonders. Although I mention fine nozzles (tubes, or tips) quite a lot, you don't actually have to use them. By snipping the very end off the bag, you can achieve a fine line of piping. Nozzles give you a slightly more polished result, that's all. Again, these are available in kitchen and sugarcraft shops everywhere. If you do want to buy nozzles, you really only need three – a couple of fine ones for piping lines and patterns (size 2 and 4) and a chunky star-shaped nozzle for piping mountains of buttercream.

Top tip for filling a large piping bag: turn the edges down and sit it in a mug and it's really easy to plop in the icing without creating havoc. When filling a small piping bag, use a teaspoon, or a little palette knife to fill the bag. Only fill the bag a third full, otherwise, when you fold the top over, the icing squidges out all over your hands.

# Sugar paste and fondant

Right now, pay attention please. Sugar paste is sometimes called "rolled fondant". It is not the same as marzipan, but is of a similar consistency, and comes in a solid form. If you buy something in a tub which is soft and spreadable, take it back.

Fondant icing is made with powdered icing sugar which generally has had some dried glycerine added to it. You need to get this in powder form. It is available in lots of supermarkets.

If you are looking in a bewildered manner at the shelves of the supermarket and you are wondering whether to buy anything which calls itself "ready-made frosting", "ready to use royal icing" and generally comes in a tub, step away. If you are not sure, just buy a box of ordinary icing (confectioner's) sugar and make glacé icing.

# Hens and Eggs

I realize it may be rather unexpected to dedicate a whole section to eggs, but it's worth it. Believe me.

It's quite difficult to make a cake without eggs. Which leads us on to that tricky old question: which came first? The chicken or the egg? As far as I am concerned, the answer is simple – the chicken. Every time. It may strike you as curious that I am so interested in eggs and chickens. Well, I am interested in eggs only up to a certain point. I want them to be fresh, with a large, orange, deeply flavoured yolk. More importantly, I want to know that the hen that laid the egg has been allowed to roam around outside, scratching and pecking and generally behaving like a happy, healthy hen. I want to know that the hen had access to hedges or trees that she could hide under (should she wish) and room enough to run, flapping her wings like a loon in the attempt to catch a particularly juicy invertebrate.

I have wanted to keep chickens for years, and it was only within the past four years that we have lived in a house with a garden big and safe enough to keep a small flock of truly free-range hens. When we moved, our old neighbours gave us a hen house as a moving-in present. How cool is that? So, where to get the chickens?

Living in the countryside, it seems that every village has someone who is trying to offload another half-dozen chicks, as well as the "posh" hen breeders who produce exquisite specimens of poultry perfection – grand, colourful, proud chickens that strut around posing. I had wondered about stripy Marans or a few Light Sussex, and always had a soft spot for the amazingly huge Buff Orpington. But, driving through a local village,

I stopped at the notice board and saw a poster advertising the Battery Hen Welfare Trust (BHWT). Decision made then and there. Phone call made. Hens booked.

These hens are not "liberated" from a battery in some sort of balaclava'd storming. The BHWT does not condemn battery egg farmers – they are not doing anything against the law and they are producing the cheap eggs that the public demands. Most farmers aren't against the idea of switching their production to free-range – if it is economically viable. The only way this is going to happen is if consumers demand free-range eggs, not only on the shelves but also in all food products that contain eggs. So, next time you reach for that "value" pack of eggs and nice cheap egg sandwich, have a think about "values", eh? Lecture over.

I sort of love and hate getting new hens. When we arrive, the barns are carpeted with pale, bald creatures. They are all huddled on top of each other and crammed into a corner. This is behaviour of their own making. There is room for them to move, but it would appear that they have become so used to being crammed up against each other that they continue to do so. Hens are picked up and toenails cut. Long, curled claws that have never felt a solid floor or been used to scratch have never worn down and so overgrow. Quick pedicure over, the rather startled bird is then placed in one of the boxes with a chum for comfort and packed into the car.

The journey home is usually quiet, the hens sitting still and silent in their new cages. Then we arrive home and things get exciting. The hen house has always been given a bit of a spring clean and a really thick bed of lovely fresh straw. If there are already resident hens, they will be waiting in the run. The only time I keep the hens in their (massive) run is when new girls arrive. They stay in the run together for ten days while they get

My rescued hens came from The Battery Hen Welfare Trust. The BHWT is a registered charity. For more information and contact details visit: www.thehenshouse.co.uk

to know each other and the new girls learn how to go to bed at night.

The old girls do not tend to welcome the new girls with open wings. There's a lot of "I was here first ... hey, ugly...no, you can't be in our gang ... ha, ha, ha, look at *her*!" It's called sorting out the pecking order. The new girls stand still for a few moments, then creep around lifting their legs carefully and wondering just how dangerous bare earth is. They rarely stand on two legs, as if having both feet on firm ground is just too much of a sensory overload. There may be some trial pecking at the ground and preliminary attempts at flapping, but on the whole it really is a very sorry sight. Their combs are huge and pale, their chests and bottoms are bald, and their wings are often featherless. We are truly talking "oven-ready". That evening you must go and find all the hens who know that it is getting dark and they want to go to sleep, and so head for the nearest hedge. One by one, you scrabble in the hedge and pick up the sleepy hens and pop them in the hen house. After three nights of this, they decide to go to bed themselves. Hoorah!

Two days after they have arrived in their new home, the girls are running, flapping, clucking, scratching and pecking. Proper hen behaviour. A few months later, they are fat, brown, feathered and definitely pampered pets, loitering at the back door, telling me that they're coming over all faint because of their lack of food. A scrap of bread (or cake) would be just the job, then they'll feel much better, thank you very much.

Hens make jolly good pets. I've never heard of a dangerous hen running amok and causing fear and panic. Granted they do steal food out of your hands and are terrible time-wasters. If you don't want hens – and you may not – *please* buy free-range eggs, whether you are making cakes or not.

# Low-faff

These cakes are deliciously low-maintenance – in other words, low-faff. Really easy. I mean it.

I have suggested two sorts of icing. The first is glacé icing made with water or lemon juice. It's a question of sieving the icing (confectioners') sugar, adding the liquid and stirring. That's it. The second icing is butter-cream. Butter, sieved icing sugar. Stir (albeit quickly in a beating-type manner). Flavours, colours and embellishments may be added, but they are a doddle. You'll see the recipes for the basic icings at the beginning of the chapter.

Even more of a doddle is plonking some-thing on top a cake straight out of a jar or tub. Why not? Nutella, lemon curd, mascarpone, whipped double cream – all absolutely delicious and simply divine (darling) on top of a cupcake.

I feel I should point out that low in faff doesn't actually mean low in cost. An Extremely Posh Rose Cupcake is really quite extravagant – those roses don't come cheap. Hey-ho. All worth it in the world of cupcake exquisiteness, I say.

There is a bit of very basic piping in this chapter, but I still think this counts as low-faff. It's not difficult and doesn't justify getting all fidgety and worried about. Really. I promise.

# Glacé icing

This is the simplest and most useful icing. Minimum ingredients and minimum fuss. Very easily correctible if you make it too thick or too thin.

✳ Makes enough for 12 cupcakes

200 g/7 oz/1¼ cups icing (confectioners') sugar, sifted
juice of 1 large lemon OR
    55 ml/2 fl oz boiling water
gel food colouring of your choice

Put the sifted icing sugar in a bowl. Add the liquid slowly, a little at a time, and stir until smooth. Stop adding liquid when you like the look of the consistency. It should be a smidgen thicker than double (whipping) cream.

Add a tiny amount of colour – use a cocktail stick (toothpick) dipped into the colour. You can always add more if you want, but there is no way to undo a lurid amount of colour without making a super-huge batch of icing.

# Royal icing

This is a great icing for piping. It's not that tricky, but you need to watch the consistency. An icing that hold peaks like a stiff meringue is what you need.

✳ Makes enough for 24 cupcakes

2 large free-range egg whites
500 g/1 lb 2 oz/about 3¼ cups icing (confectioners') sugar, sifted
2 tsp freshly squeezed lemon juice

Put everything into a large mixing bowl, and whisk away for 4–5 minutes until the mixture is very white and standing in stiff peaks. It should be really quite stiff. If the mixture is too cement-like, add a few drops of lemon juice or boiling water. If it is too runny, add a little more sifted icing sugar.

This makes a lot of icing, so you may wish to halve the quantity, but it does keep well for around a week in the refrigerator if you seal it really well. I put a layer of cling film (plastic wrap) on top of the surface, then seal in an airtight plastic container.

# Buttercream

Another classic and easy icing. Needs no drying time and can be coloured and flavoured very easily. It does freeze well if you find you've got leftovers.

✳ Makes enough for 12 cupcakes

225 g/8 oz/1½ cups icing
  (confectioners') sugar, sifted
100 g/3½ oz/scant ½ cup soft
  unsalted butter
½ tsp vanilla essence (optional)

Beat everything together in a large bowl for a few minutes until light and fluffy. If the mixture looks a little on the heavy side, ½ teaspoon boiling water whisked in works wonders.

If you want coloured or flavoured buttercream, add away to your heart's content (see suggestions below).

## Coffee
Add 1 teaspoon very, very, *very* strong espresso or filter coffee (made with instant coffee – 3 teaspoons coffee granules with just enough boiling water to make it liquid). Mix through thoroughly.

## Chocolate
Add 2 teaspoons sifted cocoa powder to the buttercream mixture. If you want it more chocolatey, add more. If you are feeling very extravagant, melt 60g (2 oz) good-quality dark (at least 70% cocoa solids) chocolate in a bowl over a pan of simmering water, and add that, too. Mix through thoroughly.

## Lemon
Add the grated zest of 1 unwaxed lemon and 2 teaspoons freshly squeezed lemon juice. Mix through thoroughly. This works well with lime, too. And orange, come to that.

# Your basic no-mucking-around cupcake

This is the ultimate low-faff cupcake. Personally, I like to see a variety of sprinkles and sweets (candies), but I have a cupboard full of alternatives, which makes life easier. You can even choose from a great selection of sprinkly pots that have four different types of sprinkles in one pot. Enjoy. Incidentally, this sort of cake was a firm favourite with my all-time best ever hen, the very wonderful Jean.

*Makes about 12

110 g/4 oz/1 cup self-raising flour, sifted
110 g/4 oz/½ cup caster (superfine) sugar, sifted
110 g/4 oz/½ cup margarine, softened
1 tsp baking powder
2 large free-range eggs
1 tsp pure vanilla extract
1 quantity of glacé icing (p.16)
sweeties (candies) and sprinkles, to decorate

*You will find these pictured on pages 20-21.*

## TOP TIP:

Always sieve the flour and sugar – it doesn't take long and makes all the difference, believe me.

Preheat the oven to 160°C/325°F/Gas mark 3. Line a 12-hole muffin tin (pan) with cupcake cases (baking cups). Put all the ingredients (except the icing and sprinkles, of course) in a mixer (food processor, food mixer, or just a big bowl with an electric whisk). Mix really well until the mixture (batter) is light and fluffy.

Plonk heaped teaspoons of the mixture into the prepared cases, and bake in the oven for about 20 minutes until golden, and firm and springy when you give them a light prod on top. Let them cool before preparing the icing – on a wire rack if you want, but not 100 per cent necessary.

To make the icing, you really must sift the icing sugar. Add the water really slowly (a teaspoonful at a time), and stir until you have a consistency like thick double (whipping) cream. Pour a little icing on top of each cake, and add whatever decoration takes your fancy before the icing dries.

# Buttercream mountain

This cupcake is exactly the same as the basic cupcake and the rather impressive mountainous swirl is simplicity itself. Should the idea of piping get you a bit hot and bothered, fret not. Just smear a thick layer of buttercream over the cake with a knife. It will still be wonderful.

✻ Makes about 12

110 g/4 oz/1 cup self-raising flour
110 g/4 oz/½ cup caster (superfine) sugar
110 g/4 oz/½ cup margarine, softened
1 tsp baking powder
2 large free-range eggs
1 tsp pure vanilla extract
1 quantity of buttercream (see p.17)
food colouring (optional)
sprinkles (optional), to decorate

✻ You will need a large piping (decorating) bag with a star nozzle (tube)

✻ You will find these pictured on page 15.

✻ VARIATION:

If you want to make lemon cupcakes, omit the vanilla extract and add the finely grated zest of a lemon.

Preheat the oven to 160°C/325°F/Gas mark 3. Line a 12-hole muffin tin (pan) with cupcake cases (baking cups). Sift the flour and sugar into a large mixing bowl, food processor or food mixer. Add the margarine, baking powder, eggs and vanilla, and beat until the mixture (batter) is really pale and fluffy. Plop heaped teaspoons of the mixture into the prepared cases, and bake in the oven for about 20 minutes until golden and firm to the touch.

While the cakes are in the oven, you can get on with the buttercream. Put the softened butter in a big bowl and sift in the icing (confectioners') sugar (don't try getting away with not sifting the sugar – I can almost guarantee you will be wailing over a horrid gritty, lumpy mixture). Beat the living daylights out of it all till it's lovely and light.

Add whatever flavouring you want – a few drops of vanilla or some lemon juice – and the merest dab of colour from the end of a cocktail stick (toothpick). If the mixture is a bit too stiff, add a teaspoon boiling water and beat away.

When the cakes are cool, put a star nozzle (tube) into a piping (decorating) bag. If you put the piping bag into a mug or tumbler, it is much easier to fill. Plonk the buttercream into the piping bag and swirl away. Gild the lily with sprinkles, sweeties (candies) or drizzles of syrupy sauces.

# Your classic butterfly cake

Who doesn't love these cakes? They are easy-peasy, and I think look fantastic. You can go for completely plain butterfly cakes with unadorned buttercream, but that would be not quite in the spirit of this book. Colour the buttercream – oh, go on, you know you want to.

❋ Makes about 12

1 quantity of basic cupcakes
    (see p.18)
1 quantity of buttercream
    (see p.17)
gel food colouring of your choice
icing (confectioners') sugar for
    dusting (optional)

❋ *You will find these pictured on
pages 20-21.*

Have your cooked cupcakes at the ready. Decide how many colours you are going for, and divide the buttercream into the appropriate number of bowls. Tint the buttercream with tiny dabs of colour.

With a small, sharp knife, cut the central portion out of the top of the cake. I like to delve down a bit so that you end up with an almost conical-shaped lid. Set the "lids" aside. Plonk some buttercream into the hole left by your delving. You could pipe it in, but the extra washing up then means that this recipe may qualify for an extra faff point.

Cut each lid in half and "place delicately" (more plonking) on top of the buttercream in the manner of a butterfly about to fly off. For a bit of extra finesse, dust the tops of the cupcakes with icing sugar. Purely optional and, if you are in true low-faff mode, you certainly won't bother.

# Basic extremely low-faff square cakes

Well, this is a right old humdinger. Later in the book it gets beautifully faffy, messing about with all sorts of complications. These little dollops are really easy. It's a tray bake. Sshhh. Don't tell anyone.

✳ Makes about 12 if you can be bothered to put them in cases (baking cups)

110 g/4 oz/1 cup self-raising flour
110g/4 oz/½ cup caster (superfine) sugar
110g/4 oz/½ cup margarine, softened
1 tsp baking powder
2 large free-range eggs
1 tsp pure vanilla extract
1 quantity of glacé icing (see p.16)
gel food colouring of your choice
sprinkles of your choice, to decorate

✳ You will find these pictured on pages 20-21.

Preheat the oven to 160°C/325°F/Gas mark 3. Grease and line a 20-cm/8-in square baking tin (pan).

Sift the flour and sugar into a large mixing bowl, food processor or mixer. Add the margarine, baking powder, eggs and vanilla. Turn on or beat like fury until it's all pale and fluffy. Tip the mixture (batter) into the prepared baking tin and level carefully. Bake in the centre of oven for about 20 minutes or until the cake is firm to the touch and golden. Cool on a wire rack.

Make the icing (see p.16). You now have two options here. For both options, you need to have the cake upside down so that the bottom of the cake is the part that's iced. If the top of the cake is not level, just level it by slicing the uneven bit off with a sharp knife so that the cake sits flat.

**Option one** means that you cover the whole cake in icing, add the sprinkles and cut into squares when the icing is dry. Place each square in an individual case (baking cup).

**Option two** involves cutting the cake into squares first, then drizzling the icing over the individual squares so that the icing dribbles down the sides of the cakes, too. Add the sprinkles and, when the icing is dry, place the squares in cases.

# Carrot cupcakes with honey orange cream cheese frosting

There are so many recipes for carrot cake around that I'd say, if you have a favourite one, try it in cupcake cases (baking cups). This is my favourite – one of those recipes on a scrappy bit of paper tucked into my collection. I like the fact that the frosting contains no sugar, being sweetened with honey. One thing I would suggest – use only proper cream cheese – sometimes sold as curd cheese. I've never had much success with the white soft cheese sold in supermarkets everywhere. It's too runny.

✳ Makes about 10

175 g/6 oz/1 cup soft brown sugar
175 ml/6 fl oz sunflower oil
3 large free-range eggs
150 g/5 oz/1¼ cups plain (all-purpose) flour
1½ tsp bicarbonate of soda (baking soda)
1½ tsp baking powder
1 tsp ground cinnamon
½ tsp freshly grated nutmeg
pinch of salt
225 g/8 oz/1¼ cups grated or shredded carrot

**For the cream cheese frosting**
1 x 225 g/8 oz packet cream cheese (not soft or light cream cheese), softened
2 tsp honey (or more to taste)
grated zest of 1 unwaxed orange
orange sprinkles, to decorate

Preheat the oven to 180°C/350°F/Gas mark 4. Line a 12-hole muffin tin (pan) with cupcake cases (baking cups). Mix the sugar and oil in a large bowl. Add the eggs and mix well. Sift in the dry ingredients, and beat everything together until really well combined. Next add the grated carrots and stir through well.

Place spoonfuls of mixture (batter) in the prepared cases, and bake in the oven for 15–20 minutes. Watch these like a hawk, as they have a tendency to burn. If the tops are getting a bit dark and it looks like the innards are still raw, cover with greaseproof paper or baking parchment, and cook a little longer. Remove from the oven and allow to cool.

While they are cooling, make the frosting. Put the cream cheese in a bowl, and beat until softened. Stir in the honey and orange zest. Give it a taste to make sure it is sweet enough. Add a bit more honey if you want. When the cakes are cold, spread the frosting over the top and decorate at will.

# Lemonylicious

I love lemony things. So do lots of other people, it would appear. Home-made lemon curd is gorgeous, but I purposely haven't included a recipe as that would certainly not count as low-faff. There are some really good jars of lemon curd available, and I would urge you to splash out on a really fine one, rather than the scary luminous stuff that you have to cut your way through. The crème fraîche is optional, but I think the combination is just delicious. This recipe is used throughout the book where lemon cupcakes are called for – just leave out the lemon curd and crème fraîche.

✳ Makes about 12

110 g/4 oz/1 cup self-raising
    flour
110 g/4 oz/½ cup caster
    (superfine) sugar
110 g/4 oz/½ cup margarine,
    softened
1 tsp baking powder
2 large free-range eggs
grated zest of 2 large unwaxed
    lemons, plus extra shreds, to
    decorate (optional)
1 tbsp freshly squeezed lemon
    juice
1 x 350 g/12 oz jar lemon curd
200 ml/7 fl oz crème fraîche

Preheat the oven to 170°C/325°F/Gas mark 3. Line a 12-hole muffin tin (pan) with cupcake cases (baking cups).

Sift the flour and sugar into a large bowl, food processor or mixer. Add all the other ingredients except the lemon curd and crème fraîche, and beat until light and fluffy.

Place heaped teaspoonsful of the mixture (batter) in the prepared cases, and bake in the oven for about 20 minutes until firm to the touch and golden. Remove from the oven and allow to cool.

Once cool, use a small, sharp knife to slice the top off each cake, place a generous spoonful of lemon curd on top of the cake and put the lid back on.

Top the whole shebang with a dollop of crème fraîche and a few tiny shreds of lemon zest if you wish.

# Coffee and walnut cupcakes

Another classic. These are firm favourites, even though they are distinctly lacking in gaudiness. I love the old-fashionedness of them – that and the fact that they are absolutely delicious.

✳ Makes about 12

110 g/4 oz/1 cup self-raising
    flour
110 g/4 oz/½ cup caster
    (superfine) sugar
110 g/4 oz/½ cup margarine,
    softened
1 tsp baking powder
2 large free-range eggs
3 tbsp instant coffee granules
    diluted in 1½ tbsp boiling
    water
50 g/2 oz/scant ½ cup chopped
    walnuts, plus 12 walnut halves
    for decoration

**For the icing**
200 g/7 oz/⅓ cup icing
    (confectioners') sugar, sifted
2 tbsp instant coffee granules
    diluted in 2 tbsp boiling water

Preheat the oven to 170°C/325°F/Gas mark 3. Line a 12-hole muffin tin (pan) with cupcake cases (baking cups).

Sift the flour and sugar into a large bowl, food processor or mixer. Add the margarine, baking powder and eggs, and beat really well until pale and fluffy. Add 1 tablespoon of the coffee mixture. This may be enough – don't add the rest if you don't need to. You don't want the mixture (batter) to be too liquid. Fold in the chopped walnuts, and spoon the mixture into the prepared cases. Bake in the oven for about 20 minutes until firm to the touch. Remove from the oven and allow to cool.

To make the icing, put the icing sugar in a bowl. Add the very strong coffee bit by bit. If the mixture is too stiff, add a few more drops of boiling water. If the coffee flavour is too strong for you, do dilute the mixture to your taste. Spoon the icing over the cooled cupcakes, and dot the top of each one with a walnut half.

# Black Forest
## gateau cupcakes

Now, I am not ashamed to say that I have a huge fondness for kitsch. I love things such as avocado and prawns, scampi in a basket and small things lined up on cocktail sticks or toothpicks. So it really should come as no surprise that Black Forest gateau should make an appearance. These things might not be fashionable, but, by George, they taste good.

✳ Makes about 12

85 g/3 oz/¾ cup self-raising flour
4 tbsp cocoa powder
110 g/4 oz/½ cup caster (superfine) sugar
110 g/4 oz/½ cup margarine, softened
1 tsp baking powder
2 large free-range eggs
1 x 450 g/1 lb jar black cherry jam
200 ml/7 fl oz double (whipping) cream, whipped
60 g/2 oz dark (bittersweet) chocolate (at least 70% cocoa solids), grated
glacé cherries, to decorate (optional)

Preheat the oven to 170°C/325°F/Gas mark 3. Line a 12-hole muffin tin (pan) with cupcake cases (baking cups).

Sift the flour, cocoa powder and sugar into a large bowl, food processor or mixer. Add the margarine, baking powder and eggs. Beat well until the mixture (batter) is light and fluffy. Spoon the mixture into the prepared cases, and bake in the oven for about 20 minutes until firm to the touch.

Remove from the oven and allow to cool.

Once cool, smother the top of each cupcake with a generous amount of the jam – you could also use a jar of cherries that have been soaked in kirsch, yum, yum – then pile the whipped cream on top. Finish with some grated dark chocolate. And a cherry on a cocktail stick (toothpick), if you dare.

# Chocolate Maltesers cupcakes

How can anyone not love this? So easy.

* Makes about 12

85 g/3 oz/¾ cup self-raising
  flour
4 tbsp cocoa powder
110 g/4 oz/½ cup caster
  (superfine) sugar
110 g/4 oz/½ cup margarine,
  softened
2 large free-range eggs
1 tsp baking powder
2 tsp milk
1 x 400 g/13 oz jar of Nutella or
  other chocolate hazelnut
  spread
bag of Maltesers or other
  chocolate malted milk balls
  (size depends on your
  generosity)

Preheat the oven to 170°C/325°F/Gas mark 3. Line a
12-hole muffin tin (pan) with cupcake cases (baking cups).

Sift the flour, cocoa powder and sugar into a large bowl,
food processor or mixer. Plonk in all the cake ingredients
and whisk away until pale and fluffy (use an electric whisk
if you are using a large bowl). Plop heaped teaspoons of the
mixture (batter) into the prepared cases, and bake in
the oven for around 20 minutes until firm and springy
to the touch. Remove from the oven and allow to cool.

Once cool, spread Nutella on top of each cupcake, then
place Maltesers on top. You can be as generous as you
want. If you want to create a veritable tower (and why
wouldn't you – unless you've eaten them all already?),
use a splodge of Nutella to glue the Maltesers together.

# Banana cupcakes with cream cheese frosting

Banana cake is another classic yummy treat that translates really well to a cupcake. I find that this cake is usually very sweet, so I like to add a little zing with lime zest and, rather than make a sugary icing, top them with a cream cheese frosting, which also adds a little sharpness. The frosting here does contain sugar, but, if you wish, you could easily make the frosting from the Carrot Cupcakes recipe (p.24) and add lime zest instead of orange.

\* Makes about 12–15, depending on size of bananas

250 g/9 oz/1 cup plus 2 tbsp butter
225 g/8 oz/1 cup caster (superfine) sugar
2 large free-range eggs
3 large ripe bananas, mashed
375 g/13 oz/3¼ cups self-raising flour
75 ml/2½ fl oz milk
grated zest of 1 lime
1 tsp lime juice
dried banana chips (optional), to decorate

**For the cream cheese frosting**
250 g/9 oz/4 cups icing (confectioners') sugar
125 g/4½ oz/generous ½ cup cream cheese
grated zest and juice of 1 lime

Preheat the oven to 180°C/350°F/Gas mark 4. Line a 12-hole muffin tin (pan) with cupcake cases (baking cups).

Whisk the butter and sugar together until really pale and fluffy. Add the eggs and continue to whisk. The mixture will curdle at this stage – I've never known it not to. Don't worry about it. Add the bananas and then sift the flour on top, and fold it in. Add the milk and lime zest and juice, and fold again until everything is incorporated.

Bake in the oven for 20–25 minutes until firm on top and golden brown.

While the cupcakes are in the oven, make the frosting. Sift the icing sugar over the cream cheese and beat well. Add the zest and the juice, if needed, but don't let the frosting get too runny.

Once the cupcakes have cooled, smother them with the frosting and top with a dried banana chip, if using.

# Ginger and lemon cupcakes

This is from the "grown-up" fold, but children do like them! It's just that there is a distinct absence of glitter and colouring, and a general lack of over-the-topness. How peculiar.

✳ Makes about 12

110 g/4 oz/1 cup self-raising flour
110 g /4 oz/½ cup caster (superfine) sugar
110 g/4 oz/½ cup margarine, softened
1 tsp baking powder
1 tsp ground ginger
grated zest and juice of 1 unwaxed lemon
2 large free-range eggs
50 g/2 oz crystallized (candied) ginger, chopped, plus extra, to decorate
200 g/7 oz/1⅓ cups icing sugar, sifted

Preheat the oven to 170°C/325°F/Gas mark 3. Line a 12-hole muffin tin (pan) with cupcake cases (baking cups).

Sift the flour and sugar into a mixing bowl, food processor or mixer. Add the margarine, baking powder, ground ginger, lemon zest and eggs. Beat well until light and fluffy. Fold in the chopped crystallized ginger. Spoon the mixture (batter) into the prepared cases, and bake in the oven for about 20 minutes until golden and firm to the touch. Remove from the oven and allow to cool.

Make the icing by slowly adding the lemon juice to the icing sugar and mixing well. If you need a little more liquid, add a few drops of boiling water. You are looking for the consistency of thick soup.

When the cakes are cool, spoon the icing over and top with a little chunk of the extra ginger.

# Easy-peasy heart cupcakes

Yes, there is some piping here. No, it isn't tricky. Royal icing is invaluable for piping. You can use it for icing cakes if you like a very hard surface. What I suggest you do if you are a bit nervous about your piping skills is to practise on a plate or directly onto your work surface. When you are happy that you have the flow of the shape right, go for it! Let the base layer of icing dry really well before you start piping. If you want to pipe something other than hearts, do it. Tiny spots all over look really pretty and couldn't be simpler.

✳ Makes around 12

1 quantity of basic cupcakes (see p.18)
1 quantity of glacé icing (see p.16)
2 tbsp royal icing (see p.16)
food colourings (preferably gel)

✳ *You will need a parchment piping (decorating) bag*

Make the cupcakes as for the recipe on p.18, and allow them to cool.

To make the glacé icing, sift the icing sugar into a bowl, and add the water drop by drop until you get the consistency you require (thick soup). Add the food colouring, and check that you still have the correct consistency – you may need to add a little more sifted icing sugar. Spoon the icing over the cakes and leave to dry. Leaving them for a couple of hours at this stage is really good, if you can.

Tint the royal icing with the food colouring, then use some to fill the parchment piping (decorating) bag, squeezing the icing down to the end.

Snip the very end off the bag. Practise piping the hearts or whatever shape you want, then pipe away to your heart's content on the top of each iced cupcake (geddit?). Leave to dry for another hour or two before scoffing.

# Grown-up mocha cupcakes

The coffee in the buttercream makes these a bit more adult, and the sponge has that slight hint of bitterness that is needed to cut through all that topping. I think that you will find that most very grown-up and sensible people who wouldn't usually think about eating a cupcake will be like putty in your hands if you offer them these.

\* Makes about 12

85 g/3 oz/³/₄ cup self-raising flour
4 tbsp cocoa powder
110 g/4 oz/½ cup caster (superfine) sugar
110 g/4 oz/½ cup margarine, softened
1 tsp baking powder
2 tbsp instant coffee granules dissolved in 2 tsp boiling water
2 large free-range eggs
25 g/1 oz chocolate coffee beans (optional)
gold dragees (optional), to decorate

**For the mocha buttercream**
110 g/4 oz/½ cup unsalted butter, softened
225 g/8 oz/1½ cups icing (confectioners') sugar
1 tbsp cocoa powder
1 tbsp instant coffee dissolved in 2 tsp boiling water

\* *You will need a large piping (decorating) bag fitted with a star nozzle (tube)*

Preheat the oven to 170°C/325°F/Gas mark 3. Line a 12-hole muffin tin (pan) with cupcake cases (baking cups).

Sift the flour, cocoa and sugar into a mixing bowl, food processor or mixer. Add the margarine, baking powder, dissolved coffee and eggs, and beat well until the mixture (batter) is light and fluffy. (If you want to add a real bonus feature, chuck in a small handful of chocolate coffee beans and fold them in.) Spoon the mixture into the prepared cases, and bake in the oven for around 20 minutes until firm to the touch. Remove from the oven and allow to cool.

To make the buttercream, put the butter in a bowl. Sift the icing sugar and cocoa over the top, and beat away. Add the coffee and beat again. If the mixture is too wet, add a bit more sifted icing sugar. Bit dry? Add a tiny bit more coffee.

Place a piping (decorating) bag with a star nozzle into a beaker, and fill the bag with the icing. Pipe huge, glamorous swirls onto the cakes, and dot with gold dragees, if you so wish.

# Extremely posh but nevertheless low-faff rose cupcakes

Now, these aren't cheap, but, heavens to Betsy, they look good, don't they? I make quite a lot of these, and I do still feel slightly embarrassed when people go all gooey over them. I mean, they can't realize that this is the ultimate in "plonking" cakes. Again, I say to you: sssssssshhhhh. These cakes could also be made in lemon by following the recipe for the lemon cupcakes on p.26 and omitting the lemon curd, and also making up the icing with lemon juice, rather than water.

✳ Makes about 12

1 quantity of basic cupcakes
  (see p.18)
200 g/7 oz/1⅓ cups icing sugar,
  sifted
boiling water
gel food colouring
12 sugar (candied) roses

Make the cupcakes as for the recipe on p.18, and allow them to cool.

To make the icing, put the icing sugar in a bowl, and slowly add boiling water until you have a thick soup consistency. Add the food colouring and pour over cakes. Wait about 10 minutes before carefully placing (plonking) a rose on top of each cupcake.

*Voilà.*

✳ TOP TIP:

These sugar roses are made from flower paste (essentially a sugar paste that dries very hard) and can be bought from sugarcraft shops. They are readily available from on-line sugarcraft shops in a variety of colours and sizes.

# Cupcakes with mascarpone and fruit

This recipe works really well as a dessert after a lovely summery lunch. You can make it with either vanilla or lemon cupcakes – both delicious. This is another of those recipes that can look staggeringly beautiful, but is criminally easy.

✳ Makes about 12

1 quantity of basic cupcakes
   (see p.18) or lemon cupcakes
   (see p.26)
250 g/9 oz mascarpone cheese
selection of soft ripe fruit such
   as blueberries, strawberries,
   raspberries, peaches
   and nectarines

Make the cupcakes as for the recipe on p.18 or p.26, and allow them to cool.

Empty the tub of mascarpone cheese into a bowl and give it a bit of a beating, but don't add anything to it. Place a dollop of mascarpone on top of each of the cupcakes, and artfully arrange the fruit on and around the cakes.

✳ VARIATION:
If you are using lemon cakes, add a little lemon curd to the mascarpone, top the cakes with this, then spoon over passion fruit pulp.

# Mid-faff

2

Things get slightly more elaborate in this chapter, but I would argue that a) they are worth it and b) they aren't beyond anyone who doesn't mind spending more than 20 minutes in the kitchen. Glitter is used liberally, edible glue gets a look-in and sugar paste (rolled fondant) also appears.

Even if you are hopeless at drawing, there are plenty of artistically beautiful cakes on offer here. Cut out a star or heart from sugar paste and smother it in glitter. The end result is dazzling.

This chapter also gets a bit more adventurous with the actual body of the cupcake – a flourless and fatless sponge (surely this must count as health food ...?), cakes inspired by chocolate brownies, and Battenburg(ish) cupcakes.

Chocolate ganache appears in this chapter, not because it is difficult, but because occasion-ally it can misbehave and split (like mayonnaise).

A final word about sugar paste: when stuck onto an icing such as glacé or fondant, it does have a tendency to get very shiny and wet after a day or two. Still edible, but the consistency does change. I'd advise you *not* to store cupcakes with sugar paste somewhere airtight (the icing keeps the cakes fresh for a few days anyway) and eat them as quickly as you can.

# Cupcakes à la Battenburg

I love the colour combination of Battenburg and toyed with the idea of wrapping the whole caboodle in marzipan, but I settled on this version. I like the tang of the apricot jam, but you could use any other flavour. You don't have to stick to pink sponge, either. Why not green and blue?

Makes about 24

220 g/8 oz/2 cups self-raising flour
220 g/8 oz/1 cup caster (superfine) sugar
220 g/8 oz/1 cup margarine, softened
2 tsp baking powder
4 large free-range eggs
2 tsp pure vanilla extract
pink food colouring (preferably gel)
apricot jam for spreading
1 quantity lemon glacé icing (p.16)
dolly mixture or other sprinkles, to decorate

Preheat oven to 160°C/325°F/Gas mark 3. Grease two 20cm/8 in square cake tins (pans), and line with baking parchment.

Sift the flour and sugar into a mixing bowl, food processor or food mixer. Add the margarine, baking powder, eggs and vanilla. Beat until light and fluffy. Divide the mixture (batter) into two equal portions in separate bowls, and add a little bit of pink food colouring to one half. Pour each cake mixture into a separate tin, and bake in the oven for 20–25 minutes until firm to the touch and golden. Don't worry that the pink cake doesn't look very pink. Remove from the oven and turn both cakes onto wire racks to cool.

Using a sharp knife, level the tops of the cakes so that the top and the bottom are completely flat. Spread a thin layer of apricot jam over the upper side of the pink layer. Place the plain cake on top so that the bottom side of the sponge faces upwards. Cut into 2 cm/¾ in strips.

Now, pay attention. Lay one strip on its side so that you have a line of pink and a line of yellow. Spread a thin layer of jam over the top. Take another strip of cake and lay it on its side on top of the jammy strip, but reversed so that pale lies directly on top of pink and vice versa. Cut these strips into squares, and drizzle with the glacé icing. Let some of the icing dribble down the sides. Plop a dolly mixture (or alternative adornment) on top, and place in cupcake cases.

# A lemony little-bitta-glitta

Discovering edible glitter was a high point in my cake decorating life. It really is fantastic stuff. And what's more, what goes in, must come out, as glitter is poorly absorbed by the body ... need I go on? Of course, you needn't stick to hearts. Go with whatever shape takes your fancy. Go mad with colour and glitter. It's what it's there for.

* Makes about 12

1 quantity of lemon cupcakes
    (see Lemonylicious, p.26)
cornflour (cornstarch)
    for dusting
sugar paste (rolled fondant)
edible glue
edible glitter
food colouring (preferably gel)
1 quantity lemon glacé icing
    (p.16)

* *You will need a heart-shaped pastry cutter and a small clean paintbrush*

Make the cupcakes as the recipe on p. 26, and allow to cool.

Dust a work surface or clean board with cornflour (cornstarch) and knead a piece of sugar paste (rolled fondant) the size of a golf ball until it softens and becomes pliable. Dust a rolling pin with some more cornflour, and roll out the sugar paste until it is about 3 mm/$\frac{1}{8}$in thick.

Cut out 12 hearts (or as many cakes as you have) using a heart-shaped pastry cutter, and brush them lightly with edible glue. Tip a pile of glitter onto a plate, and carefully lower the hearts glue-side down onto the glitter. Carefully lift off so that you have a completely glitter-covered heart. Place onto another cornflour-dusted plate, right-side up, and continue with the others.

Make the glacé icing (see p.16) and tint whatever colour you choose, and spoon the icing over the cakes. Let both the icing and the glitter hearts dry out. The hearts are much easier to handle if they've been given a bit of air.

Put a tiny blob of edible glue on the centre of each cake, and carefully place (no plonking, please) a heart on top. Beautiful.

# Lemony lustres

Now, with this cake I have used the traditional way of making a Victoria sponge, which is why I have included it in the mid-faff section. It's not tricky – just slower than the bung-it-all-in method I love so much. Edible lustre comes as a powder in tiny tubes from sugarcraft shops.

✳ Makes about 12

110 g/4 oz/½ cup butter, softened
110 g/4 oz/½ cup caster (superfine) sugar
2 large free-range eggs, beaten
110 g/4 oz/1 cup self-raising flour, sifted
1 tsp baking powder
grated zest of 1 unwaxed lemon
1 tbsp freshly squeezed lemon juice

**For the decoration**
1 quantity glacé icing (p.16)
gel food colouring (optional)
1 tbsp royal icing (see p.16)
edible lustre (available from cake decorating and sugarcraft shops)
½ tsp vodka or other clear alcohol

✳*You will need a small paintbrush*

Preheat the oven to 170°C/325°F/Gas mark 3. Line a 12-hole muffin tin (pan) with cupcake cases (baking cups).

Cream the butter and sugar together until really pale and fluffy. Slowly add the beaten eggs, beating well after each addition. Sift the flour and baking powder onto the mixture (batter) and, using a large metal spoon, carefully fold it in. Add the lemon zest and, if the mixture looks a little stiff, add the juice a little at a time (it may not be necessary). Fold again. The mixture should gently plop off the spoon. Spoon into the prepared cases, and bake in the oven for 20–25 minutes until golden and firm to the touch. Remove from the oven and allow to cool.

Make the glacé icing (see p.16) and colour as required. Spoon over the cooled cakes. When the icing has dried, put the royal icing into a piping (decorating) bag with a fine nozzle (tube), and pipe a large heart onto each cupcake. Wait for this to harden slightly – around an hour.

To finish, tip ½ teaspoon of the lustre onto a saucer or into a small bowl. Add some vodka to the lustre drop by drop. Mix with the paintbrush until you have a consistency just a tiny bit looser than a paste. Leave the alcohol to evaporate – the mixture will thicken up slightly. Carefully brush the lustre mixture over the piped heart and let it dry.

# Bite my cherry

Yes, yes, this is my version of the cherry Bakewell tart, one of my all-time favourite cakes. But, get this – no fat, no flour and contains fruit and nuts. Not only is it perfectly wonderful for gluten-intolerant personages, but also it must somehow count as "good for you". Surely?

✳ Makes about 12

4 large free-range eggs, separated
175 g/6 oz/¾ cup caster (superfine) sugar
225 g/8 oz/2¼ cups ground almonds
1 tsp baking powder (or ½ tsp bicarbonate of soda (baking soda) and 1 tsp cream of tartar if you want to keep it gluten-free)
12 glacé (candied) cherries

**For the decoration**
1 quantity lemon glacé icing (p.16)
golf ball-sized piece of sugar paste (rolled fondant)
red food colouring (preferably gel)
edible glue
red edible glitter
green food colouring (preferably gel)
1 tbsp royal icing (see p.16)

✳ *You will need a parchment piping (decorating) bag*

Preheat the oven to 200°C/400°F/Gas mark 6. Line a 12-hole muffin tin (pan) with cupcake cases (baking cups).

Beat the egg yolks and sugar together until pale. In a clean, dry separate bowl, whisk the egg whites until stiff peaks form. Gently fold them into the egg yolk mixture, then fold in the ground almonds and baking powder. Spoon the mixture (batter) into the prepared cases, and push 1 cherry down into each sponge. Bake in the oven for 15–20 minutes, keeping an eye on them throughout – burnt almond doesn't taste good. Remove from the oven and allow to cool.

Make a glacé icing (p.16) and pour a little over each cake. While you are waiting for the icing to set (30 minutes), make the sugar paste cherries. Dye the sugar paste red by dipping a cocktail stick (toothpick) into the red food colouring and transferring it to the paste. Knead the colour in evenly, then make little cherry-sized balls (one for each cupcake), paint them with the edible glue and roll them in the edible glitter.

When the icing is dry, add a little food colouring to the royal icing to make it green. Fill a parchment piping (decorating) bag with the royal icing, squeezing the icing down to the end. Snip the very end off the bag. Stick a sugar paste cherry onto each cupcake with a tiny blob of edible glue, and pipe green stalks and leaves with the green royal icing.

# Choc-a-doodle-do

This is my version of a chocolate brownie. It is not, however, as heavy as a brownie. There's something unappealing about picking up a cupcake and being able to use it as a doorstop. It's wrong. So I've just taken the key elements of the brownie: chocolate, nuts, chocolate and chocolate.

❋ Makes about 12

4 large free-range eggs, separated
150 g/5 oz/1⅔ cups caster (superfine) sugar
3 tsp cocoa powder
225 g/8 oz/2¼ cups ground almonds
1 tsp baking powder
50 g/1¾ oz/scant ½ cup chopped mixed nuts (such as hazlenuts, walnuts, almonds)
small bag of Maltesers or other chocolate malted milk balls

### For the chocolate ganache
2 x 100 g/3½ oz bars of good-quality dark (bittersweet) chocolate (at least 70% cocoa solids)
200 ml/7 fl oz double (whipping) cream

Preheat the oven to 200°C/400°F/Gas mark 6. Line a 12-hole muffin tin (pan) with cupcake cases (baking cups).

Whisk the eggs and sugar together until pale and creamy. In a clean separate bowl, whisk the egg whites until stiff peaks form, then gently fold into the egg yolk mixture. Sift over the cocoa and fold in with the almonds, baking powder and chopped nuts. Lightly bash half the packet of Maltesers – you want large chunks, rather than powder – and fold these into the mixture. Spoon the mixture into the prepared cases, and bake in the oven for 15–20 minutes.

Make the ganache by putting the chocolate, still in its wrapper, onto a hard surface. Grab a rolling pin and smash the living daylights out of that chocolate. Open it all up carefully over a bowl and, hey presto! Gravel chocolate. Just make sure none of the wrapper goes in with the choc.

Heat the cream in a small heavy saucepan until almost boiling, then pour over the chocolate. Leave for 30 seconds before gently stirring it all together. Carefully spoon the ganache on top of the cupcakes, and top each one with a leftover Malteser if you haven't eaten them all. There probably won't be enough for all the cakes, so you might as well eat them …

# No-nonsense chocolate on chocolate

When I want a cupcake, this tends to be one I go for. It hits all the right spots. Moist, dark chocolatey sponge and a thick layer of almost fudge-like dark chocolate ganache on top. Stand with your eyes closed as you savour every last morsel. Feel those endorphins releasing themselves.

Makes about 12, but you may choose to say that there were only 6

60 g/2 oz/½ cup self-raising flour
60 g/2 oz/½ cup good-quality unsweetened cocoa powder
1 tsp baking powder
110 g/4 oz/½ cup caster (superfine) sugar
110 g /4 oz/½ cup margarine, softened
2 large free-range eggs
2 tbsp milk
150 g/5 oz good-quality dark (bittersweet) chocolate (at least 70% cocoa solids)
100 g/3½ oz good-quality milk chocolate
200 ml/7 fl oz double (whipping) cream

Preheat the oven to 160°C/325°F/Gas mark 3. Line a 12-hole muffin tin (pan) with cupcake cases (baking cups).

Sift the flour, cocoa, baking powder and sugar into a large bowl, food processor or mixer. Add the margarine and eggs, and beat away until light and fluffy. I think it's worthwhile to stop the mixer after a few moments and scrape everything down the sides of the bowl, so that you know none of the cocoa gets stuck. Beat again. If the mixture looks quite stiff, add enough of the milk and beat, so that you get the mixture (batter) plopping nicely off a spoon. Spoon into the prepared cases, and bake for 20 minutes, or until firm on top. Let the cakes cool and get on with the ganache.

Bash all the chocolate to smithereens as in Choc-a-doodle-do (opposite). (If the chocolate is not still in its packet, do this between two pieces of greaseproof or waxed paper.) Tip into a bowl. Put the cream in a small heavy saucepan and bring it to the boiling point, then pour over the chocolate. Leave for 30 seconds before gently stirring it all together. (This ganache differs slightly in that I've fiddled with the ratio of chocolate to cream, and added a smidgen of milk chocolate.) Spoon the ganache over the top of the cupcakes. Embellish as you wish.

Mid-faff

# Love letters

Cupcakes were invented for declarations of love, surely? Valentine's Day is a particularly busy time for me, and the "I love you" box has become a bit of a classic. Although it looks lovely in oranges and reds, I also did a really nice one for a bloke in greens and purples.

* Makes about 12

1 quantity of basic cupcakes in
   vanilla or lemon (p.18)
1 quantity glacé icing (p.16)
red, orange and ruby food
   colouring (preferably gel)
golf ball-sized piece of sugar
   paste (rolled fondant)
cornflour (cornstarch)
1 tbsp royal icing (p.16)
edible glue

* *You will need a piping
   (decorating) bag with a fine
   writing nozzle (tube) and
   1 small and 1 tiny heart-
   shaped cutter*

Have your cupcakes ready. Make the glacé icing (p.16) and divide the mixture among three bowls. Colour each bowl with orange, ruby and red food colouring, using one colour for each bowl. Divide the sugar paste into three, and also colour these to the same intensity in their respective colours as the icing, kneading the colour in evenly. Lightly dust a work surface with cornflour (cornstarch) and roll out each of the sugar pastes until about 3 mm/⅛in thick. Cut 4 small and 4 tiny hearts out of each colour. Leave to dry on a cornflour-dusted plate for at least 1 hour.

Ice the cupcakes so that you have four each of each colour, and leave to dry. With the orange cakes, stick a large ruby heart in the middle with a small red heart on top. With the ruby cakes, stick on a large red heart with an orange tiny one. With the red cakes, stick a large orange heart with a small ruby heart. Leave overnight to dry.

Fill a piping (decorating) bag with a fine nozzle (tube) with the royal icing. Squeeze the icing right to the end. Line the cupcakes up in three rows of four, keeping the same colour in each row, so you can keep an eye on what is piped where. Pipe "I" across one cupcake, "love" across another and "you" across a third. Pipe tiny white dots all around the edge of all of the cakes, and put a central dot on all the cakes that don't have writing on. A large piped kiss wouldn't go amiss.

# Cupid's cupcakes

I have one word to say here: "silicone" – the most wonderful invention in the world of baking tins (pans). They are just fantastic. You don't need to line them or even grease them. For these cupcakes, you really do need to invest in a silicone heart-shaped muffin tray.

✳ Makes about 8

110 g/4 oz/1 cup self-raising
    flour
110 g/4 oz/½ cup caster
    (superfine) sugar
1 tsp baking powder
110 g/4 oz/½ cup margarine,
    softened
2 large free-range eggs
1 tsp pure vanilla extract
1 quantity lemon or plain glacé
    icing (p.16)
food colouring (preferably gel)
1 tbsp royal icing (see p.16)
edible lustre
vodka

✳ *You will need a silicone heart-
shaped muffin tray, metallic
foil cupcake cases (baking
cups), a piping (decorating) bag
with a fine size 2 nozzle (tube)*

✳ *Pictured here with the
Floribunda Cupcacus recipe,
see p.75.*

Preheat the oven to 170°C/325°F/Gas mark 3.

Sift the flour, sugar and baking powder into a bowl, food processor or mixer. Add the margarine, eggs and vanilla, and beat until pale and fluffy. Spoon the mixture (batter) carefully into the silicone muffin tray, place on a metal baking sheet and bake in the oven for about 20 minutes, until golden and firm to the touch. Let the cupcakes cool in the muffin tray, then turn them out onto a wire rack.

Slice the tops off the cupcakes so that you have a level surface and turn the cakes upside down. You want to ice the bottoms of the cakes. Make the glacé icing (p.16) and tint whatever colour your heart desires (sorry). Drizzle the icing all over the cakes and let it run down the sides.

Before the icing is completely dry, lay out all your metallic cupcake cases (baking cups). Dip your fingers into a bowl of cold water, then lift the cakes onto the cases – this stops the icing sticking to your fingers. Carefully mould the cases around the hearts, and the cases should stay put.

When the icing is completely dry, pipe decorations onto the cakes in royal icing. Let that dry. Mix some edible lustre with a few drops of vodka (see Lemony Lustres, p.45), and paint onto the royal icing. Alternatively, you could paint the entire top with edible glue and dip into glitter. Wooo-hooo!

# Boys' own

I like the idea of a masculine cupcake! Well, if there are cupcakes with frocks and shoes, it's only fair that the chaps should have something. Let us not forget that men are huge consumers of cake, although they may pretend they aren't that bothered. Right. The idea for these came while my son was watching the original Batman. High art indeed.

✳ Makes about 12

1 quantity of lemon or basic
    vanilla cupcakes (see p.26 or
    p.18)
1 quantity glacé icing (p.16)
gel food colouring in assorted
    colours
2 tbsp royal icing (see p.16)

✳ *You will need 3 piping*
    *(decorating) bags fitted with*
    *fine nozzles (tubes)*

Make the cupcakes according to whichever recipe you choose, and leave to cool.

Make the glacé icing with the icing (confectioners') sugar and either the lemon juice or water. Colour the icing a really deep blue or green or brown. Cover the cakes with the icing and let them dry really well. With colour this dark, it is important that the icing is as dry as possible before you start piping.

Divide the royal icing into three bowls, and tint them whatever colour the chap likes. The royal icing needs to be really firm, so if it's a bit on the loose side add a little more sifted icing sugar. Pipe on appropriately butch comic-strip-type words, such as "BIFF", "POW" and "ZAP". Word of warning: if you pipe on the words before the icing underneath has dried, or if the royal icing is too wet, the darker colour will bleed into the piping.

# A star is born

Stars are great on cupcakes. First, they look fantastic; secondly, everyone loves them; and, thirdly, they are dead easy. Marvellous. Mixing up styles of stars onto a plateful of cupcakes looks great.

✳ **Makes about 12**

1 quantity of basic vanilla or lemon cupcakes (see p.18 or p.26)
1 quantity glacé icing (p.16)
gel food colouring
golf ball-sized piece of sugar paste (rolled fondant)
cornflour (cornstarch) for dusting
2 tbsp royal icing (see p.16)
edible glue
silver dragees

✳ *You will need 3 piping (decorating) bags with fine nozzles (tubes), a star-shaped cutter and a clean paintbrush*

✳ *You will find these pictured on p.41.*

Make up the cupcakes and leave to cool. Make up the glacé icing (p.16) and divide the icing into two bowls. Leave one batch of icing white, and gently tint the other a pale blue. Ice the cakes so that half the cakes have white icing on them, while the remaining cakes are iced in blue. Leave to dry.

Tint the sugar paste (rolled fondant) with gel to an intense blue. Knead the colour in evenly. Dust a work surface with a little cornflour (cornflour), and roll out the sugar paste to about 3 mm/⅛in thick. Cut out 6 stars.

Divide the royal icing into three bowls and tint each bowl with the food colouring – you can use the same colour, i.e. blue, in different intensities, so that you end up with three distinctly different tones of blue. Put the icing into three separate piping (decorating) bags with fine nozzles (tubes), pushing the icing down to the end of each bag.

Place a blob of edible glue on three of the white cakes and three of the blue cakes, and stick a star to each. Take the palest royal icing and pipe a blob into the middle of the star. Place a dragee on top of the blob.

For the other cakes, pipe a 5-pointed star with whatever colour you like. Pipe five dots between the outer points of the star in another colour. Using the most intense colour, pipe a small circle in the centre of the star. Fill in the circle with contrasting icing, then finally add a tiny blob of the third colour to the top.

# Mid-faff insects

I say "mid-faff" because there are also "high-faff" insects. I don't think I have an unhealthy preoccupation; it's just that insects lend themselves to cupcake embellishment extremely well.

* Makes about 12

1 quantity of lemon or basic
    vanilla cupcakes (see p.26 or
    p.18)
1 quantity glacé icing (p.16)
golf ball-sized piece of sugar
    paste (rolled fondant)
gel food colouring
cornflour (cornstarch)
    for dusting
edible glue
1 tbsp royal icing (see p.16)
coloured dragees (optional)

* You will need butterfly cutters
    and 2 or 3 piping (decorating)
    bags with fine nozzles (tubes)
    (depending on how many
    colours you want to use)

Make the cupcakes according to whichever recipe you choose, and leave to cool. Make the glacé icing (p.16) and colour as you wish. Ice the cakes and leave to dry.

To make the butterflies, tint some of the sugar paste (rolled fondant) with the food colouring. Knead the colour in evenly. Lightly dust a work surface with cornflour (cornstarch) and roll out the paste until it is about 3 mm/⅛in thick. Cut out the butterflies and leave to dry for 30 minutes or so.

Meanwhile, you can get on with the ladybirds. Tint some sugar paste red, and another very small amount black. Knead both balls separately until the colour is even. Depending on how big you want the ladybirds to be, roll a ball of red paste into a body-type shape. Take a tiny bit of black, and flatten it to make a face. Stick it on one end. Make two tiny sausages of black to make the wing edges. Then make some really tiny balls for the spots. How many spots you manage will depend on how fine your handiwork. Two seems to be my limit ... Poke a little face into the black with the end of a cocktail stick (toothpick), and make some tiny white antenna with white sugar paste.

Everything can be stuck on with edible glue. When the little chap is finished, stick him on the cake and use a little royal icing in a piping (decorating) bag with a fine nozzle (tube) to
(continued on p.60)

(continued from p.59)
surround him with a few piped flowers for company.

Back to the butterflies, stick them onto the cakes with some edible glue. Tint several little batches of royal icing and, using decorating bags fitted with fine nozzles, you can then pipe patterns on the butterfly's wings. Add dragees if you wish. I think these cakes look great with spots piped round the edge of the cake and a dragee popped on the top of each spot.

# Butterflies go disco

I have developed a growing stash of cutters. The glitter butterfly remains a firm favourite.

✳ Makes about 12

1 quantity of basic vanilla or lemon cupcakes (p.18 or p.26)
1 quantity glacé icing (p.16)
food colouring (preferably gel)
cornflour (cornstarch) for dusting
golf ball-sized piece of sugar paste (rolled fondant)
edible glitter
edible glue

✳ *You will need butterfly cutters (large, small or both) and a paintbrush*

Make the cupcakes according to whichever recipe you choose, and leave to cool.

Make up the glacé icing (p.16) and colour as you wish. Pour over the cakes and leave to dry.

Dust a little cornflour onto a work surface, and roll out the sugar paste (rolled fondant) until it is about 3 mm/$\frac{1}{8}$in thick. Cut out butterflies – allow one large butterfly per cake or two small.

Brush a little edible glue all over the butterflies and dip onto the edible glitter that you have poured onto a plate.

Stick the butterflies to the cakes. If you are using two small ones, it looks lovely if you have them flying off in different directions.

# Mysteries from the deep

None of these would stand up to close scrutiny from a marine biologist, but we won't worry about that. Very popular with smallish children, these ones. It's one way to get them to eat fish, I suppose.

Makes about 12

1 quantity of lemon or basic
   vanilla cupcakes (see p.26
   or p.18)
1 quantity glacé icing (p.16)
2 tbsp royal icing (p.16)
gel food colouring in assorted
   colours
silver dragees (optional –
   not suitable for very small
   children)

*You will need three or four
piping (decorating) bags with
fine nozzles (tubes)*

Make the cupcakes according to whichever recipe you choose, and leave to cool.

Make the glacé icing (p.16) and colour it using the gel food colouring. I think blue or green really works best for these cakes. Ice the cakes and leave to dry.

Meanwhile, divide the royal icing into three or four small bowls, and tint them whatever colour you like. Put the icing in piping (decorating) bags with fine nozzles (tubes), and practise on a plate if you aren't 100 per cent confident. A starfish is really easy to start with – a five-pointed star, filled in with tiny dots. Add a face with different-coloured icing and you're done. Fishes can be outlined, then scales and face filled in with other colours. An octopus looks great with random tiny dots around the body and edging onto the tentacles.

Don't make the designs all the same – have three or four different fish as well as an octopus or a starfish. No rules, just get piping.

# Cut-out classics

Cutting shapes out of coloured sugar paste (rolled fondant) is simplicity itself, and the results look great. This recipe is in this chapter only because of the various stages needed – there really is no skill involved at all. Unless you are colour blind, in which case get someone to help you.

✳ *Makes about 12*

1 quantity of any sort of cupcake
    except for chocolate
1 quantity glacé icing (p.16)
gel food colouring in assorted
    colours
golf ball-sized piece of sugar
    paste (rolled fondant)
cornflour (cornstarch) for
    dusting
1 tbsp royal icing (see p.16)
edible glue

✳ *You will need various cutters,*
   *several piping (decorating) bags*
   *with fine nozzles (tubes) and*
   *a paintbrush*

Make the cupcakes according to whichever recipe you choose, and leave to cool.

Make the glacé icing with icing (confectioners') sugar and the lemon juice or boiling water, and divide into as many bowls as you want colours. Tint the icing with the food colouring, then ice the cakes. Leave to dry.

Separate the sugar paste (rolled fondant) into as many colours as you want and tint them. Knead the colour in evenly. Dust a work surface with cornflour (cornstarch), and roll out the sugar paste until it is about 3 mm/$\frac{1}{8}$in thick. Cut out whatever shapes you like. I usually do hearts, stars and flowers. Leave to dry for about 30 minutes.

Using edible glue, stick a cut-out shape onto a cake of a different colour. Keep going until all the cakes have a shape.

Tint the royal icing into as many colours as you like and, using a piping (decorating) bag with a fine nozzle (tube), pipe a blob onto the middle of each sugar-paste shape. I think it's nice to have a third colour appear on the cake at this point. You may also like to pipe tiny dots all the way round the edge of the cake.

# High-faff

# 3

Welcome to the truly wonderful world of faffdom.
These are cakes that sometimes can take days to
make (only because you have to make some of the
decorations in advance). There is some serious
fiddling and twiddling, but if I am honest, nothing
that requires any particular skill. This is clearly
difficult for me to confess, but it's true. I am
actually very cack-handed, but don't mind
spending stretches of time making little petals
that two days later can be individually stuck onto
a cake. I should get out more.

Just remember, although it may take a total of
three days to make the cupcake, it will still only
take fifteen seconds to eat. If this worries you,
either take a photo and build a shrine to the
memory of your work or slap a bit of Nutella on a
cake and throw on some Maltesers. If it doesn't
worry you, embrace the faff and welcome to my
wonderful world ...

# Fondant icing

I am starting this chapter with a general introduction to fondant icing, as it is the lovely, glossy, shiny basis for all the cakes' preliminary icing. You can buy boxes of fondant icing (confectioners') sugar in big supermarkets and some sugarcraft shops. We are talking about a powdered product here, *not* to be confused with solid blocks of sugar paste (sometimes called "rolled fondant"). Not the same thing at all.

175 g/6 oz/1½ cups fondant
    sugar
55ml/2 fl oz boiling water or
    lemon juice

As for glacé icing, just mix the ingredients together, but this time you want a really stiff, almost dough-like consistency. I put it in the mixer with the dough hook, much easier.

Place in the top of a double boiler, or in a bowl over a pan of barely simmering water. GENTLY heat. Don't let the water boil; if the fondant gets too hot, it loses its lovely shiny appearance. As it warms, it gets runnier.

If the fondant is getting warm and melting a bit, but is still very stiff, add a bit more liquid and stir until it looks a bit looser, like very thick cream.

I find it easier to take it off the heat at this stage and transport dollops into separate bowls to add colour. It will stiffen up again quite quickly, just add a few drops (literally) of water to loosen it up. The consistency you want to end up with is thick, thick soup. Actually, even cheese sauce-like! Lump-free, of course.

# Incredible invertebrates

May I present high-faff dragonflies and bees.

✳ Makes about 12

1 quantity of lemon or basic
   vanilla cupcakes (see p.26
   or p.18)
1 quantity of fondant icing (p.68)
gel food colourings
golf ball-sized piece of sugar
   paste (rolled fondant)
edible glue
edible glitter
1 tbsp royal icing (see p.16)
dragees for the bees' eyes

✳ *You will need a paintbrush,
   a cocktail stick (toothpick), a
   piping (decorating) bag with
   a fine nozzle (tube) and a
   steady hand*

✳ *You will find these pictured
   on p.61.*

Make the cupcakes in whichever recipe you choose. Allow to cool, then cover with fondant icing, tinted in colours of your choice. Let the icing dry completely.

Make the dragonfly wings first. Tint some of the sugar paste (rolled fondant) whatever colour you want the wings, kneading the colour in evenly. Take pea-sized pieces and roll them into tiny sausages and flatten them slightly. You will need 2 top wings per dragonfly. You also need 2 slightly smaller bottom wings (petit pois) made the same way. Cover the wings in edible glue, and roll them in glitter. Leave to dry for at least 1 hour.

To make the glittery bumble bee, tint some of the sugar paste a deep yellow and a small amount black. Knead the colour in evenly. Take broad (fava) bean-sized pieces of the yellow paste, and roll into cylinder shapes with rounded ends. Cover in glue and roll in gold glitter. To make the yellow bee, do the same, but omit the glitter. Leave to dry. Make tiny black stripes and glue them over the bees. Make a tiny black sting and stick it to the bee's bottom. Again leave to dry.

Make some tiny white sugar-paste wings and glue them to the top of the bee using a tiny dab of edible glue. For the faces, make two indents with a cocktail stick (toothpick), and pop in some dragees. Draw a smile with the cocktail stick.

Stick the bees onto the cakes using edible glue, and pipe on a couple of flowers using royal icing. (continued on p.70)

Back to the dragonflies. Stick 2 large top and 2 small bottom wings onto a cake. For the body, tint some royal icing a contrasting colour and pipe a thickish line between the wings, starting at the top of the wings and ending well below the bottom wings. At the top of the wings, pipe an extra blob for the head. Stick 2 dragees on for eyes. Stick the dragonflies onto the cakes using edible glue, then pipe any flowers or dots in royal icing around the cupcakes to finish them off.

# Blinking butterflies

These butterflies don't blink. The reason they are called "blinking" is that they can sometimes break. But the time and effort you put in should hopefully reward you with a really pretty snazzy invertebrate.

✳ Makes about 12

a little white vegetable fat (vegetable shortening) such as Trex or Crisco
3 tbsp royal icing (see p.16)
food colouring (preferably gel)
1 quantity of cupcakes of your choice
1 quantity of fondant icing (see p.68) or chocolate ganache (see p.50) if you are using chocolate cakes

✳ *You will need a sheet of clear acetate and 2 parchment piping (decorating) bags with fine nozzles (tubes)*

You need to make the butterflies at least 2 days in advance, preferably even earlier. Draw the outline of the butterfly's wings on a piece of paper, and repeat so that the whole sheet is covered in butterfly wings. Place the acetate over the paper and wipe over a very thin layer of white vegetable fat.

With 2 tbsp of the royal icing, tinted whatever colour you want the wings to be, fill a piping (decorating) bag with a fine nozzle (tube) and push the icing to the end. Use the icing to pipe round the outline of the individual wings. Loosen up some of the icing with a few drops of water so that it is the consistency of double (whipping) cream. Carefully fill in the wings with this mixture, and leave to dry for 2–3 days. In addition, pipe two tiny strips on the acetate for each butterfly, which will be their antennae.

*You will find these pictured on p.67.*

Make the cupcakes and fondant or ganache according to their recipe and ice the cakes. Let the icing dry.

Place the remaining royal icing (white or coloured) into a parchment piping bag and snip the end off the bag. This icing is going to be the body of the butterfly. Pipe quite a fat line down each cake, just longer than the inside wing of the butterfly. Pipe a little extra blob at the top for the head.

Extremely carefully, peel each wing off the acetate. You may find a small, flexible palette knife (metal spatula) helps here. Place each wing on the edge of the body you have just piped. If you can manage it, you can position the wings on the body at an angle so it looks as if they are about to take off. Trying not to mutter too much, peel off the antennae and stick them on the top of the butterfly's head. It's always worth making a few extra antennae in case they break ...

**TOP TIP:**

Don't attempt these if you are in a hurry - you need to make the butterflies at least 2-3 days in advance.

# Bollywood

There is a cake maker called Peggy Porschen who has been a huge influence on me. I love her work; it's witty, beautiful, very clever and her cakes look delicious. My Bollywood cakes are taken from an idea that I saw in her book *Pretty Party Cakes*. Her ideas about clashing colours, glitter and general over-the-topness hit all the right buttons. I salute her.

✱ Makes around 12

1 quantity of lemon cupcakes
   (see Lemonylicious p.26)
1 quantity of fondant icing
   (see p.68)
golf ball-sized piece of sugar
   paste (rolled fondant)
gel food colouring in assorted
   colours
cornflour (cornstarch)
   for dusting
1 tbsp royal icing (see p.16)
edible glitter (any colour to
   match your scheme, plus
   green for the leaves)
edible glue
edible lustre in gold
vodka

✱ *You will need 1 large and*
   *1 small press-in rose mould,*
   *1 press-in leaf mould,*
   *2 parchment piping (decorating)*
   *bags and a paintbrush*

Decide on your colour scheme, and separate the sugar paste (rolled fondant) into four pieces. Using the gel food colouring, tint three of the pieces different reds or purples or whatever colours you want the flowers to be. Tint the fourth piece green. Knead in the colour so that each one is even.

Dust the moulds liberally with cornflour (cornstarch), and make 6 large roses, remembering to re-dust between pressing each flower. Continue the process, using the other moulds and dusting between each use, so that you end with 12 leaves and between 18 and 30 small flowers as well, depending on how committed you are!

Brush each rose lightly with edible glue and dust a little bit of glitter over each one. Do the same with the leaves with green glitter. Leave to dry out for around 24 hours.

Make the cupcakes as per the recipe on p.26, preferably in gold foil cupcake cases (baking cups) for the full-on Bollywood look. Remove from the oven and allow to cool. Meanwhile, make the fondant up following the method on p.68. Divide the mixture into as many bowls as you want colours. Really intensely colour the icing, making sure the colour is even mixed in, and pour the icing onto the cakes.

(The number of cakes you ice in each particular icing obviously depends on how many different colours you have.) Allow the icing to dry for at least 1 hour, preferably longer.

Carefully decide on your placement of the roses and stick to the cakes using edible glue. If you are using 2 leaves and a large rose, put the leaves on first, then the rose on top. If using the small flowers, decide whether you want three or five, and how you want them arranged before you commit yourself to gluing them in place.

Tint two-thirds of the royal icing the same green as the large leaves, and put into a parchment piping (decorating) bag with no nozzle. Squeeze the icing right to the end, then with very sharp scissors cut a small V shape out of the bottom of the bag. Practise piping on a work surface, and you will see that you are able to pipe tiny leaves. Dot a few of these around the small rose posies.

Next put the remaining white royal icing into a parchment piping bag, and snip just the very end off. Pipe small dots around the cakes, in groups or singly, as you wish. Leave to dry.

Mix a small amount of lustre on a saucer with a drop or two of vodka until you have a consistency like emulsion paint (quite thick). Carefully brush each of the white spots with the lustre. Allow them to dry.

They're done.

# Floral faffdom

Clearly not the quickest way to make flowers, but I like the result. I don't think these are as difficult as the butterflies, but they are quite time-consuming. Great!

Makes about 12

white vegetable fat (vegetable shortening) such as Trex or Crisco
2 tbsp royal icing (see p.16) plus extra 1 scant tbsp for flower centres
food colouring (preferably gel)
1 quantity of cupcakes of your choice
1 quantity of fondant icing (see p.68) or chocolate ganache (see p.50) if you are using chocolate cakes
edible glue

*You will need a sheet of clear acetate, a couple of parchment piping (decorating) bags and a fine paintbrush*

*You will find these pictured on p.67.*

Cover a sheet of paper with petal templates (and leaves if you want to do leaves, too). Place the acetate over the paper, and wipe over a very thin layer of white vegetable fat. Decide what colour you want the flowers to be, and colour the 2 tbsp royal icing accordingly. Using a parchment piping (decorating) bag with the very end snipped off, pipe round the edges of the petals and leaves.

Thin out the rest of the coloured icing with a little water until it is the consistency of double (whipping) cream and carefully fill in the petals and leaves. Leave to dry for 2 or 3 days at least.

Make the cupcakes in whichever recipe you choose. Allow to cool, then cover with fondant icing or chocolate ganache as required. Let the icing or ganache dry completely.

Very carefully peel off the dry petals from the acetate, and stick them to the cakes with a tiny blob of edible glue under each petal. You may choose to have one flower per cake or a veritable posy. Add leaves as required.

Colour the small amount of extra royal icing whatever colour you want the centre of the flowers to be. Using a parchment piping bag with the very end snipped off, pipe a small blob into the centre of each flower and leave to dry.

# Floribunda cupcacus

These roses can look very pretty, or completely over the top and vulgar. It really depends on the size, colour and the free hand with the glitter that transforms the flower from tasteful to trashy. I know which I prefer ...

Makes about 12

golf ball-sized piece of sugar paste (rolled fondant)
gel food colouring in assorted colours
cornflour (cornstarch) for dusting
edible glitter (optional)
1 quantity of lemon or basic vanilla cupcakes (see p.26 or p.18)
1 quantity of fondant icing (see p.68)
edible glue

*You will find these pictured on p.55.*

Make the roses first, the day before if possible. Separate the sugar paste (rolled fondant) into as many portions as you want colours and tint with the food colouring. Knead the colour in evenly. Lightly dust a work surface with cornflour (cornstarch). Take a marble-sized piece of sugar paste and divide it in two. Take one piece and roll it into a small fat sausage. On the work surface, flatten in slightly and try to keep one long edge a bit thinner than the other longer edge. Repeat with the other piece. Start rolling one sausage up, with the thinner layer being the "top" of the rose. Just before you finish rolling, insert the second flattened sausage under the flap of the first one and keep rolling. Voila! You should have a rose type flower. You'll probably find that it is a bit cylindrical with a lumpy bottom. Leave the rose sitting up on its lumpy bottom for an hour or two, then slice the bottom off with a sharp knife. Continue making roses until you go mad.

If you want a glittery rose, tip some edible glitter onto a saucer and lightly dip the top of the rose in the glitter – you shouldn't need any glue. Leave to dry for at least 4 hours.

Make the cupcakes in whichever recipe you choose. Allow to cool, then cover with fondant icing, tinted with a colour of your choice. Let the icing dry completely. Carefully stick a small blob of edible glue under each rose, and place on the cupcakes, either individually or in a mixed posy.

# Women's essentials

I do believe that I am not the only female to show a passing interest in shoes, frocks and handbags. There is something rather wonderful about eating a cupcake adorned with a beautiful shoe. Not the same as actually buying a new pair and stroking them in their box, but cheaper. AND you don't have to go through the whole "Oh, no! I've had these for ages. Don't you remember?" routine.

* Makes about 12

1 quantity of lemon, basic vanilla or coffee cupcakes (see p.18, p.26 or p.27)
1 quantity of fondant icing (see p.68) (made with coffee if using coffee cakes)
2 tbsp royal icing (see p.16)
dark brown and pink gel food colouring

* You will need two piping (decorating) bags with fine nozzles (tubes)

Make the cupcakes in whichever recipe you choose. Allow to cool, then ice with pale pink fondant icing (or coffee fondant if using coffee cupcakes). Leave to dry for at least 1 hour.

Tint half the royal icing dark brown. If it gets too runny, add some more sifted icing (confectioners') sugar. Put the brown icing in a piping (decorating) bag with a fine nozzle (tube) and the remaining white royal icing into another one.

With the brown icing, pipe 1950-style dresses onto a few cakes (small waists, big skirts), high heeled shoes on a few more and handbags onto yet more. If you are stuck for ideas, look in a few magazines or draw out a few examples first. Fill in patterns and fold on the dresses, buckles and pockets on the bags, and stitch lines and other frivolities on the shoes with the white icing.

# Paisley

This is one of those designs that translates really well into all colour schemes. I've made them in blue and pink pastels, lurid limes and purples, and quite autumnal browns and oranges. This means that they can be adapted to suit all ages, genders and occasions. Handy. They aren't tricky, but do require quite a few piping (decorating) bags on the go at any one time, hence their position in the high-faff section of the book.

✳ Makes about 12

1 quantity of lemon or basic vanilla cupcakes (see p.26 or p.18)
1 quantity of fondant icing (see p.68)
3 tbsp royal icing (see p.16)
gel food colouring in assorted colours

✳ *You will need 3 or 4 piping (decorating) bags with fine nozzles (tubes), depending on how many colours you wish to use*

Make the cupcakes according to whichever recipe you choose, and allow to cool.

Make the fondant icing and separate into three or four bowls and tint accordingly. Ice the cakes with the fondant icing and leave to dry for at least 1 hour.

Decide on the actual pattern you want to pipe. You can either go for it directly onto the cake or draw it out first. Start with a large, swirling paisley shape, then it's up to you. I think you need at least three colours within the pattern, and there needs to be outer embellishment and a distinct central part.

# Very fanciful fondants

Fancy a fondant? The answer has to be yes. I will admit that these really are the high priestess of faff. But they're blooming lovely and I think worth pushing the boat out for. Don't make them for people who use food as fuel. I can't think of anything worse than someone scoffing one while talking about something entirely irrelevant and not even acknowledging that they are consuming your culinary slave labour. I'd cry.

*Makes about 16

sugar-paste (rolled fondant) roses, either rolled (see p.75) or pressed (p.72)
1 quantity of tray-bake recipe (see Basic Extremely Low-Faff Square Cakes p.23)
2 tbsp apricot jam
icing (confectioners') sugar for dusting
500 g/1 lb 2 oz marzipan
250 g/9 oz/2½ cups fondant sugar
juice of 1 lemon
food colouring (preferably gel)
edible glitter
edible glue
1 tbsp royal icing (see p.16)

*You will need metallic foil cup-cake cases (baking cups) and a parchment piping (decorating) bag with a fine nozzle (tube)

Make the roses a day before you want to make the cakes and leave them dry.

Make the tray-bake cake as per the recipe on p.23, and level off the top so that it is completely flat. Turn the cake upside down, so that the bottom is facing upwards. Warm the apricot jam and pass it through a sieve. Brush the top of the cake with a thin layer of jam.

Sprinkle some sifted icing (confectioners') sugar on a work surface, and roll out the marzipan until it is about 3 mm/⅛ in thick and the same size as the square sponge. Carefully lay the marzipan on top of the jam, and smooth over to get rid of any air pockets. Trim the edges of the cake, then cut it into four strips of equal width. Cut each strip in four, so that you end up with 16 squares.

Put the squares on a wire rack over a tray. Make up the fondant by combining the fondant sugar with the lemon juice, and colour it using the gel food colouring of your choice. Add a little more lemon juice or water if you need to – the consistency should be very thick, almost dough-like. Gently

warm the fondant over a pan of hot water, but don't overheat it. You want this fondant really quite runny, so you may wish to add even more liquid at this stage. It needs to be a tiny bit thicker than double (whipping) cream, but not cheese-sauce thick. Pour the icing over each cake so that it runs down the sides and creates an awful mess in the tray you have cunningly placed below. Leave to dry for a few minutes.

Once the fondant is dry enough, lay out your cupcake cases. Slightly dampen your fingers with a little water, then put the cakes in the cases and fold the cases round so that they stick to the cakes. When the cakes are completely dry (about 1 hour), stick the roses on with a drop of edible glue.

Tint some royal icing in the colour of your choice, and use to fill a piping (decorating) bag with a fine nozzle (tube). Pipe some spots or swirls around the cakes and leave to dry.

# Savoury

Yes, savoury cupcakes. Now, before you all start screwing up your faces and making horrid gagging noises, may I just say two words? "Cheese scone." Stick with me here. The word "scone" usually conjures up images of strawberry jam and clotted cream. Yum. But prefix "scone" with "cheese", and it also says "yum". Not weird at all. When we talk about savoury cupcakes, try to think about it as a sort of muffin. Is it getting any easier? By taking the basic concept of a savoury muffin and putting it in a cupcake case (baking cup) – albeit a large one, rather than a tiddler – and having a bit of a fiddle with the toppings and innards, you can end up with a really delicious morsel.

Savoury cupcakes are also the most fantastic excuse for the world's kitschest garnishes. Where else would a tomato rose look quite so fabulous? Or a frilly radish? Joy.

For some reason, savoury cupcakes have a tendency to stick to the case. This may bother you, or it may not. If it does, I suggest you dispense with the cases altogether, grease the muffin tin (pan) really well, and the cupcakes should slide directly out. These cakes above all others really need eating within a few hours of baking.

# Courgette, feta and spring onion cupcakes

The great hunks of feta in these cupcakes are a lovely surprise. The courgette (zucchini) adds moisture and flavour, as well as beautiful flecks of green. These go well with a really piquant salsa. The batter is very stiff, almost dough-like. Don't worry and don't add more milk. The courgettes sort out the texture. Have faith.

＊Makes about 12

200 g/7 oz/scant 2 cups plain (all-purpose) flour
2 tbsp sugar
3 tsp baking powder
½ tsp salt
1 small courgette (zucchini), grated
2 spring onions (scallions), finely chopped
225 g/8 oz/1 cup ricotta cheese
150 g/5 oz feta cheese, crumbled into chunks
2 large free-range eggs, lightly beaten
110 g/4 oz/½ cup butter, melted
60 ml/2 fl oz/¼ cup milk

Preheat the oven to 200°C/400°F/Gas mark 6. Line a 12-hole muffin tin (pan) with cupcake cases (baking cups).

Sift the flour, sugar, baking powder and salt into a large bowl, and mix through well. In another bowl, mix the courgette, spring onion, ricotta, feta, eggs, melted butter and the milk. Give it a bit of a beat around, then add to the dry ingredients. The mixture (batter) will be stiff. Spoon the mixture into the prepared cases, take the worried look off your face and put them in the oven. Bake in the oven for 20–25 minutes, or until firm to the touch and golden brown. Eat warm.

# Carrot and coriander cupcakes

A sort of savoury version of the carrot cake, this one is delicious eaten warm with a smear of garlic cream cheese on top.

Makes about 12

220 g/8 oz/2 cups self-raising flour, sifted
1 carrot, grated
60 g/2 oz/½ cup grated cheddar cheese
1 small bunch of fresh coriander (cilantro), chopped, including the stalks
1 tsp ground coriander
200 ml/7 fl oz/scant 1 cup milk
125 ml/4 fl oz/½ cup vegetable oil
1 large free-range egg, beaten
garlic cream cheese (optional), to serve

Preheat the oven to 180°C/350°F/Gas mark 4. Line a 12-hole muffin tin (pan) with cupcake cases (baking cups).

Mix the flour, carrot, cheese, and fresh and ground coriander together in a bowl. In another bowl, lightly whisk together the milk, oil and egg. Add the wet ingredients to the dry, and mix as little as possible – you just want to combine the mixture (batter) into a lumpy sort of mess. Spoon into the prepared cases, and bake in the oven for 20-25 minutes until firm to the touch and golden.

Remove from the oven and, while still warm, smear the cream cheese on top (if using) and serve straight away.

# Four-cheese cupcakes

These seem to have the same universal popularity as the cheese scone. Great for children, picnics and, when made in tiny cases, as a really sweet little accompaniment to drinks. Do feel free to alter the cheeses; these are just suggestions. Blue cheeses such as Stilton and Roquefort would also be delicious.

✳ Makes about 10

50 g/1¾ oz/½ cup grated Gruyère cheese
50 g/1¾ oz/scant ½ cup grated strong cheddar cheese
50 g/1¾ oz/scant ½ cup grated double Gloucester cheese
50 g/1¾ oz mozzarella cheese, cubed
250 g/9 oz/2¼ cups plain (all-purpose) flour
1 tbsp baking powder (yes, that is right)
½ tsp salt
1 tbsp caster (superfine) sugar
1 tbsp English mustard powder (dried ground mustard)
240 ml/8 fl oz/1 cup milk
90 ml/3 fl oz/⅓ cup vegetable oil
1 large free-range egg, beaten

Preheat the oven to 190°C/375°F/Gas mark 5. Line a 12-hole muffin tin (pan) with cupcake cases (baking cups).

Reserve half of the Gruyère cheese, and mix all the rest of the cheese together. Sift the flour, baking powder, salt, sugar and mustard powder into a large bowl. Add the cheese and give it a stir. In a separate bowl, lightly whisk together the milk, oil and egg. Add this to the flour and cheese mixture, and stir until just combined. Don't worry about the lumps.

Spoon the mixture (batter) into the prepared cases, and sprinkle with the reserved Gruyère. Bake in the oven for 20–25 minutes until golden and firm to the touch. Eat warm, if you can, but these are still delicious cold.

# Ricotta and smoked salmon cupcakes

These are great at breakfast time – or maybe for brunch. The smoked salmon rose on top of a dollop of soured cream is probably unforgivable to some, but I just can't help myself.

✳ Makes about 12

75 g/3 oz/¾ cup plain (all-purpose) flour
100 g/3½ oz/½ cup polenta
½ tsp salt
1 tsp baking powder
150 g/5 oz/⅔ cup ricotta cheese
2 large free-range eggs, beaten
75 g/2½ oz/¼ cup plus 1 tbsp butter, melted
2 tbsp fresh dill, finely chopped, plus extra to garnish (optional)
4 large slices smoked salmon, cut into small strips, plus extra dill sprigs to garnish (optional)
150 ml/¼ pint soured cream or cream cheese (optional)

Preheat the oven to 190°C/375°F/Gas mark 5. Line a 12-hole muffin tin (pan) with cupcakes cases (baking cups).

Sift the flour into a large bowl. Add the polenta, salt and baking powder. Stir through well. In another bowl, mix the ricotta, eggs and melted butter. Add the dill and stir. Add the salmon strips to the ricotta mixture, and give another good old stir. Add the contents of the wet bowl to the dry ingredients, and mix just enough to combine. Don't worry about the lumps.

Spoon the mixture (batter) into the prepared cases, and bake in the oven for 15–20 minutes until firm to the touch and golden. A skewer inserted into the centre should come out cleanly when they're done. Remove from the oven and cool.

When the cupcakes are barely warm, dollop an unhealthy amount of soured cream on top (or cream cheese if you prefer), and add a smoked salmon rose made from the extra salmon – instructions below – and a touch of extra dill.

Making a salmon rose: should you want to go the whole hog, just get a strip of salmon and roll it up, teasing out the top edge as you go.

# Olive and sunblush tomato cupcakes with pesto

Sunblush tomatoes are the sweetest, juiciest morsels and now readily available in a supermarket near you. If you haven't tried them I implore you to do so. I eat them straight from the pot, but less of my disgusting habits ...

✳ Makes about 12

300 g/10 oz/2½ cups plain (all-purpose) flour
½ tsp salt
1 tbsp baking powder
275 ml/9 fl oz/1 cup plus 2 tbsp milk
2 large free-range eggs, beaten
125 g/4½ oz/½ cup plus 1 tbsp butter, melted
1 tbsp pesto
1½ tbsp black olives, pitted and chopped
1 tbsp sunblush (semi-dried) tomatoes, roughly chopped
extra olives, tomatoes and pesto, to garnish

Preheat the oven to 200°C/400°F/Gas mark 6. Line a 12-hole muffin tin (pan) with cupcake cases (baking cups).

Sift the flour, salt and baking powder into a large bowl. In another bowl, combine the milk, eggs, butter and pesto. Stir in the olives and sunblush tomato. Add the wet ingredients to the dry, and stir just enough to combine the ingredients – ignore the lumps.

Spoon the mixture (batter) into the prepared cases, and bake in the oven for about 20 minutes until golden and firm. These are best served warm with a topping of extra olives and sunblush tomatoes, and a teaspoon of pesto drizzled over.

# Parmesan and herb cupcakes

I love the look, smell and taste of fresh herbs in a savoury cupcake. If you don't like the herbs I've suggested here, do substitute others – rosemary, chives, marjoram and basil all work really well. The key here is to use fresh herbs. Step away from the dried herbs. Step away, I said.

✱ Makes about 12

250 g/9 oz/2¼ cups plain
   (all-purpose) flour
1 tbsp sugar
50 g/1¾ oz/½ cup freshly grated
   Parmesan cheese
½ tsp salt
1½ tsp baking powder
½ tsp bicarbonate of soda
   (baking soda)
75 g/3 oz fresh flat-leaf parsley,
   finely chopped
2 sprigs of fresh thyme, finely
   chopped
4 fresh sage leaves, finely
   chopped
275 ml /9 fl oz/1 cup plus
   2 tbsp milk
75 g/2½ oz/¼ cup plus 1 tbsp
   butter, melted
1 large free-range egg, beaten

Preheat the oven to 200°C/400°F/Gas mark 6. Line a 12-hole muffin tin (pan) with cupcake cases (baking cups).

Sift the flour, salt, baking powder and bicarbonate of soda (baking soda) into a large bowl. Add the chopped herbs and cheese and stir well. In another bowl, lightly whisk together the milk, butter and egg, then add to the dry ingredients. Stir just enough to combine the ingredients and ignore the lumps.

Spoon the mixture (batter) into the prepared cases, and bake in the oven for 15–20 minutes until firm to the touch and golden.

# Bacon-and-egg cupcakes

I suppose, strictly speaking, this should be called "bacon, egg and cheese", but I like the comedy value of just calling it "bacon-and-egg". This does a good job instead of bread or toast of mopping up egg yolks with your fried breakfast.

\* Makes about 9

275 g/10 oz bacon lardons or
  6 bacon rashers
75 g/2½ oz/scant ¾ cup plain
  (all-purpose) flour
1 tsp baking powder
1½ tsp English mustard powder
  (dried ground mustard)
110 g/4 oz/1 cup grated strong
  cheddar cheese
75 g/2½ oz/¼ cup plus 1 tbsp
  butter, melted
2 large free-range eggs, beaten
150 g/5 oz/⅔ cup crème fraîche

Fry the lardons in a dry heavy frying pan or skillet over a medium heat until crispy, or snip the bacon into strips and fry until crispy. Drain on kitchen paper and set aside.

Sift the flour, baking powder and mustard powder (ground mustard) into a large bowl and stir in the cheese. In another bowl, lightly whisk together the crème fraîche, eggs and butter. Stir in the reserved bacon, then add this mixture to the dry ingredients. Stir just enough to combine, ignoring the lumps.

Spoon the mixture (batter) into the prepared cases, and bake in the oven for around 15 minutes until golden and firm to the touch. Eat warm.

# Muesli cupcakes

I know these aren't savoury, but they do go hand in hand with the bacon-and-egg cupcakes. These were inspired by a recipe by Felicity Barnum-Bobb in her book *100 Magnificent Muffins and Scones*. Please don't be put off by the large list of ingredients; I've included a recipe for muesli, which you don't have to use – just use anything you already have in the cupboard. Remember, though, that if your muesli has sugar in it the cupcakes are going to end up very sweet, and you may want to reduce the quantity of the other sugar in the recipe.

✳ Makes about 10

125 g/4½ oz/1¼ cups self-raising
   flour
2 tsp baking powder
75 g/2½ oz/about ½ cup soft
   brown sugar
100 g/3½ oz/about 1 cup muesli
   (recipe below)
150 ml/5 fl oz/⅔ cup milk
100 ml/3½ fl oz/scant ½ cup
   sunflower oil
1 large free-range egg
sunflower and pumpkin seeds,
   to decorate

**Muesli**
8 tbsp jumbo rolled oats
4 tbsp wheat germ
2 tbsp raisins
large handful of brazil nuts,
   roughly chopped
large handful of pumpkin seeds
large handful of sunflower seeds
1 tbsp dried apricots, chopped
1 tbsp dates chopped

Preheat the oven to 200°C/400°F/Gas mark 6. Line a 12-hole muffin tray with cupcake cases (baking cups). To make the muesli, mix everything together. That's it.

Sift the flour, baking powder and sugar into a large bowl. Add the muesli and stir through In another bowl, mix the milk, oil, egg, and pour onto the dry ingredients. Stir just enough to combine and don't worry about the lumps.

Spoon the mixture (batter) into the prepared cases, and sprinkle some pumpkin and sunflower seeds on top of each cupcake. Bake in the oven for 15–20 minutes until firm to the touch and golden.

# Seasonal 5

Heaven knows, I don't need an excuse to make cup-cakes, but they do lend themselves spectacularly well to all sorts of special occasions. Christmas, Easter, Valentine's, Halloween, Mother's Day – you name it and there will be a cupcake lurking round the corner, ready to say, "Look at me. Aren't I the most perfect specimen for this particular day?"

Fruitcake seems to be losing some of its appeal these days. A lovely moist boozy cake is just love-ly, but more often than not one is presented with a dried-out bit of brown stuff that tastes of little and needs a gallon of liquid to help it down. Not pleasant. Far be it from me to suggest that fruit wedding, Christmas and Christening cakes should be done away with. I am arguing that there is a case for an alternative. It's all about choice. A tower of cupcakes looks festive and can be decorated according to whatever is required.

A little box of cupcakes makes a wonderful present, especially if you have personalized them for the recipient. You can buy all sorts of nice boxes on the high street these days. One tip: don't stack them on top of each other. Very bad move.

In this chapter I haven't specified whether to use glacé or fondant icing. This gives you the choice as to whether to go medium- or high-faff.

# Piped Easter eggs

Mildly spiced sponge cakes decorated with Easter eggs make a fine Easter treat – if you don't like the sound of the sponge, just make them with vanilla or lemon cupcakes instead.

✳ Makes about 12

110 g/4 oz/1 cup self-raising flour
110 g/4 oz/½ cup golden caster (superfine) sugar
1 tsp baking powder
½ tsp mixed spice or pumpkin pie spice
½ tsp freshly ground nutmeg
110 g/4 oz/½ cup margarine, softened
2 large free-range eggs
grated zest of 1 unwaxed lemon
1 quantity of fondant or glacé icing made with lemon juice or water (see p.68 or p.16)
food colouring (preferably gel)
2 tbsp royal icing (see p.16)
dragees (optional)

✳ *You will need several piping (decorating) bags with fine nozzles (tubes)*

Preheat the oven to 160°C/325°F/Gas mark 3. Line a 12-hole muffin tin (pan) with cupcake cases (baking cups).

Sift the flour, sugar, baking powder and spices into a large bowl, food processor or mixer. Add the margarine, eggs and lemon zest, and beat until light and fluffy. Scrape the sides of the bowl to make sure all the lemon and spices are being mixed in, and beat again for a few moments. Spoon the mixture (batter) into the prepared cases, and bake in the oven for 20 minutes until firm to the touch and golden. Remove from the oven and allow to cool.

Make the fondant or glacé icing, and tint whatever colour you like with the food colouring (don't feel you have to stick to pastels). If using the fondant, warm slightly over a double boiler. Ice the cakes and leave to dry.

Tint the royal icing into as many colours as you like, and start piping wildly patterned Easter eggs onto the cakes using piping (decorating) bags fitted with fine nozzles (tubes). Add dragees for extra sparkle, if you like.

# Chocolate Easter eggs

We're on to chocolate here. No-holds-barred chocolate eggs on chocolate icing on chocolate cake. These are very good news in that they are a) easy, b) look fantastic, c) give you the opportunity for some serious bowl licking, and d) taste delicious. If you are feeling an extra-chocolatey yen, make them with Choc-a-doodle-do cupcakes (see p.50).

* Makes about 12

1 quantity of chocolate cupcakes
    (see p.29)
1 quantity of chocolate ganache
    (see p.50)
36 coloured chocolate mini
    Easter eggs

* *You will find these pictured
on p.95.*

Make the cupcakes as per the recipe on p.29, and allow them to cool.

Make the chocolate ganache as per the recipe on p.50, and spoon over the cakes. Let them dry for just a few minutes. Before the ganache is completely set, pop 3 eggs onto each cake. Leave them to set for a few hours before scoffing.

# Chirpy chirpy cheep cheep

I love those little fluffy yellow chicks that appear in shops just before Easter. If you don't want to do anything other than ice some cupcakes, you could stand one of these chicks on top. Just make sure that no one thinks that they are edible. Otherwise these simple piped chicks look very lovely. Pastel colours really do look better here.

* Makes about 12

1 quantity of basic vanilla or spiced cupcakes (see p.18 or p.96)
1 quantity of fondant or glacé icing (see p.68 or p.16) tinted in pastel colours with gel food colouring
2 tbsp royal icing (see p.16) plus 1 tbsp green royal icing (optional)
yellow, black and orange gel food colouring

* *You will need 3 piping (decorating) bags with fine nozzles (tubes)*

Make the cupcakes and allow them to cool. Ice the cooled cupcakes with a selection of pastel-coloured icings in glacé or fondant. Leave them to dry.

Split the royal icing into thirds. Take two-thirds and tint it yellow with gel food colouring. Fill a piping (decorating) bag with the yellow icing, and push to the end. To make a fluffy chick, pipe a chick shape onto the cake, and fill in the chick with random squiggles of yellow icing. Make sure that you go ever so slightly over your outline, so that the chick looks really fluffy. To make a flatter chick, again pipe an outline. Thin out some of the yellow royal icing with a few drops of water so that you have a consistency a bit thicker than double (whipping) cream. Carefully fill in the outline with this mixture, and leave to dry completely.

When both are dry, divide the remaining royal icing into two, and tint one portion black and the other orange. Fill two separate piping bags, one with the black and one with the orange. Pipe an eye on each chick (two if the chick is not in profile!) with the black icing, and a beak with the orange.

If you have any extra royal icing, tint it another colour (green looks good), and pipe tiny spots all the way round the outer edge of the cake.

# Gadzooks for the spooks

Black Halloween cupcakes are highly entertaining. Black icing is wonderful – it transforms your teeth and mouth at first bite. There is absolutely no room for subtlety here. You can scare the living daylights out of trick-or-treaters, by having a mouthful of cake just before you open the door. Rest assured that the colour does fade quite rapidly ...

✳ Makes about 12

1 quantity of lemon or basic
  vanilla cupcakes (see p.26
  or p.18)
1 quantity of glacé or fondant
  icing (see p.16 or pp.68)
black and orange food colouring
  (preferably gel)
golf ball-sized piece of sugar
  paste (rolled fondant)
edible glue

✳ *You will need a small
  paintbrush*

Make the cupcakes and allow to cool. Make up the glacé or fondant icing, and divide into two portions; use the food colouring to make one black and the other deep orange. Divide the cupcakes into two batches, and ice one batch black and the other batch orange. Leave them to dry. (These cakes need to be completely dry before you add anything else because of the dark colours.)

Take a third of the sugar paste (rolled fondant) and tint it black. Make a ghost by flattening out a piece of white sugar paste into the shape of a ghost and use edible glue to stick it onto a black-iced cupcake. Let the ghost trail over the edge of the cake in a ghostly manner. Take some tiny bits of black paste, and stick them on to make a ghoulish face for the ghost.

Make the spider by taking a bit of black paste the size of a broad (fava) bean, and sticking it onto an orange-iced cake using edible glue. Make as many legs as you can (8 is traditional!) out of slivers of black paste, and stick them on. I also like to add a final strip of black for the web. A face and fangs made out of white sugar paste finishes it off.

For the spooky eyes, take 2 elongated egg shapes of white paste, add black pupils and stick onto a black-iced cake.

# Firework frenzy

Is it just me or are more people having their own firework parties these days? Much as I enjoy a municipal gathering where thousands of huge fireworks are let off in spectacularly successful fashion, there is a part of me that hankers after a few unpredictable rockets zooming off into next door's garden. The inevitable pause between fireworks is always a good moment to get some food out. Sausages? Yes. Baked potatoes? Yes. Cupcakes? Definitely. Should you be of a nervous disposition and shy away from explosive devices, never fear. Stick a small, indoor sparkler into the top of the cake, turn the lights out and behold the gentle fizzing.

✳ Makes about 12

1 quantity of any sort of cupcakes
1 quantity of fondant or glacé icing (see p.68 or p.16) or chocolate ganache (see p.50)
gel food colourings
2 tbsp royal icing (see p.16)
dragees (multicoloured if possible)
edible glitter (optional)

✳ *You will need 3 or 4 piping (decorating) bags with fine nozzles (tubes)*

Make the cakes as for whichever recipe you choose, and make up the icing appropriate to the cake.

Ice the cakes – if not using chocolate, a really deep navy icing seems best to imitate the night sky. Let the icing dry really well (including the ganache).

Separate the royal icing into as many bowls as you want colours, and tint them accordingly with the food colouring. Using piping (decorating) bags with fine nozzles (tubes), pipe on whatever firework takes your fancy – Catherine wheels, rockets, shooting stars and those amazing fountains of coloured baubles all go well.

Sprinkle a tiny bit of edible glitter over them if you wish, and run free with the dragees, which may need a tiny dab of royal icing underneath them to hold them in place.

# Sparkling Christmas trees

This is really easy if you have a Christmas tree cutter.
If you haven't, just cut them out freehand.

✳ Makes about 12

110 g/4 oz/½ cup butter,
   softened
110 g/4 oz/½ cup caster
   (superfine) sugar
2 large free-range eggs
110 g/4 oz/1 cup self-raising
   flour
½ tsp ground cinnamon
½ tsp ground cloves
½ tsp ground nutmeg
½ tsp ground ginger
1 tbsp milk (if needed)
1 quantity of fondant icing made
   with lemon juice (see p.68)
gel food colouring (optional)
cornflour (cornstarch)
   for dusting
golf ball-sized piece of sugar
   paste (rolled fondant)
edible glue
edible glitter

Preheat the oven to 160°C/325°F/Gas mark 3. Line a
12-hole muffin tin (pan) with cupcake cases (baking cups).

Cream the butter and sugar together until really pale and
fluffy. Beat the eggs in a separate bowl, and slowly add
them to the butter and sugar mixture, beating well between
each addition. Sift the flour, baking powder and spices onto
the mixture, and carefully fold it all in using a large metal
spoon. If the mixture (batter) doesn't gently plop off a spoon,
add the milk and stir in. Spoon into the prepared cases, and
bake in the oven for around 20 minutes until firm to the
touch and golden. Remove from the oven and allow to cool.

Once the cupcakes have cooled, cover with the lemon
fondant icing (whatever colour you like, but white looks
nice and snowy). Let the icing dry.

Dust a work surface with cornflour (cornstarch), and roll
out the sugar paste (rolled fondant) to about 3 mm/⅛ in
thick. Cut out 12 Christmas trees, either using a Christmas
tree cutter or freehand.

Paint a thin layer of edible glue carefully over the entire
tree, and dip the tree in glitter. Put a little blob of edible glue
onto the middle of the cake and carefully place the tree onto
the cake. Continue until you have a tree on each of your
cupcakes. Leave to dry.

# Snowflake cupcakes

These are very pretty and can be jazzed up with the judicious use of dragees if a little sparkle is wanted. I really like these made with almond cupcakes – not sure why, but they just seem right.

*Makes about 12

1 quantity of almond cupcakes
  (see Bite My Cherry p.46)
1 quantity of fondant icing made
  with lemon juice (see p.68)
pale blue food colouring
  (preferably gel)
2 tbsp royal icing (see p.16)
silver dragees (optional)

*You will need 2 piping
(decorating) bags with fine
nozzles (tubes)

Make the cupcakes according to the recipe on p.46 (omitting the cherry, unless you particularly want it), and allow them to cool.

Make the fondant icing and divide it into two bowls. Tint one bowl very pale blue, and ice six cupcakes blue and six white. Let the icing dry.

Divide the royal icing into two bowls, and tint one bowl the same blue as the fondant icing. Using two separate piping (decorating) bags with fine nozzles (tubes), pipe white snowflakes onto the blue cakes and blue snowflakes onto the white cakes. If your piping is a bit random, console yourself with the fact that no two snowflakes are the same. Add silver dragees to the centre and the ends of the snowflakes, if wished. Leave to dry.

# Fruitcake

Calm down. It's not the fruitcake that you are thinking of – these are light and spongy and don't require two hands to lift one off a plate. This recipe is a spicy sponge, much like the recipe for Sparkling Christmas Trees (see p.104), but with the addition of some rum-soaked raisins and a few glacé (candied) cherries. I have piped Christmas trees on top of these, but you could add whatever you wished.

\* Makes about 12

110 g/4 oz/½ cup butter, softened
110 g/4 oz/½ cup golden caster (superfine) sugar
2 large free-range eggs
110 g/4 oz/1 cup self-raising flour
1 tsp baking powder
½ tsp mixed spice or pumpkin pie spice
50 g/1¾ oz/⅓ cup raisins, soaked in rum or brandy for 1 hour, drained
18 glacé (candied) cherries, quartered
1 tbsp milk (if needed)
1 quantity of fondant icing made with lemon juice (see p.68)
2 tbsp royal icing (see p.16)
silver dragees

\* You will need a piping (decorating) bag fitted with a fine nozzle (tube)

Preheat the oven to 160°C/325°F/Gas mark 3. Line a 12-hole muffin tin (pan) with cupcake cases (baking cups).

Cream butter and sugar together until pale and fluffy. Beat the eggs in a separate bowl, and gradually add to the butter and sugar mixture, beating well between each addition. Add the drained soaked raisins and beat well.

Sift the flour, baking powder and mixed spice onto a large plate, and toss the quartered cherries into the flour. Carefully add to the wet mixture, and fold in with a large metal spoon. If the mixture is a little dry, add the milk, so that the mixture (batter) plops gently off a spoon. Spoon carefully into the prepared cases, and bake in the oven for 20 minutes until firm to the touch and golden. Remove from the oven and allow to cool.

Once the cupcakes have cooled, make up the fondant icing and use to ice the cupcakes. Leave to dry.

Put the royal icing into a piping (decorating) bag, and pipe Christmas tree shapes onto the cakes. Add silver dragees to the trees as decorations.

# Twinkle, twinkle

Christmas, stars, glitter – they all go together so beautifully it would be insane not to have them here on a cupcake. I've used lemon cupcakes here, but it's not 100 per cent necessary. Up to you.

* Makes about 12

110 g/4 oz/½ cup butter, softened
110 g/4 oz/½ cup caster (superfine) sugar
2 large free-range eggs
grated zest and juice of 1 large unwaxed lemon
110 g/4 oz/1 cup self-raising flour
1 tsp baking powder
1 quantity of fondant icing made with lemon juice (see p.68)
cornflour (cornstarch) for dusting
golf ball-sized piece of sugar paste (rolled fondant)
edible glue
edible glitter in silver and gold

* You will need a star-shaped cutter and a paintbrush

Preheat the oven to 160°C/325°F/Gas mark 3. Line a 12-hole muffin tin (pan) with cupcake cases (baking cups).

Cream the butter and sugar together until really pale and fluffy. Beat the eggs in a separate bowl, and gradually add them to the butter and sugar mixture, beating well between each addition. Add the lemon zest and beat well.

Sift in the flour and baking powder, and fold in with a large metal spoon. If the mixture (batter) needs loosening a bit, add a little lemon juice. The mixture should gently plop off a spoon. Spoon the mixture into the prepared cases, and bake in the oven for 20 minutes until firm to the touch and golden. Remove from the oven and allow to cool.

Once cool, make the fondant icing and use to ice the cupcakes. Leave to dry.

Dust a work surface with cornflour (cornstarch), and roll out the sugar paste (rolled fondant) until it is about 3 mm/⅛in thick. Cut out 12 star shapes using a star-shaped cutter.

Paint edible glue over each star, making sure they are completely covered, before dipping 6 stars in gold glitter and 6 in silver glitter. Dab a tiny blob of edible glue on the centre of each cupcake and carefully place a star on top.

# White Christmas

These have got to be the ultimate in good taste. No colour and a tiny smidgen of silver. I wish I could hate them, but I don't. The marzipan addition is completely optional.

* Makes around 12

1 quantity of lemon cupcakes
  (see Twinkle Twinkle, opposite)
350 g/12 oz marzipan
icing (confectioners') sugar for
  dusting
2 tbsp apricot jam
1 quantity of fondant icing made
  with lemon juice (see p.68)
cornflour (cornstarch) for
  dusting
golf ball-sized piece of sugar
  paste (rolled fondant)
edible glue
silver dragees

* *You will need 2 star-shaped
  cutters, one smaller than
  the other, and a round cutter
  the same size as your
  lemon cupcakes*

Make the cupcakes and allow them to cool.

Put the apricot jam into a small saucepan and warm over a gentle heat, then push the jam through a fine sieve to remove any lumps. Brush the jam over the cakes.

Sprinkle some icing (confectioners') sugar over a work surface, and roll out the marzipan to about 3 mm/⅛in thick. Using a round cutter the same diameter as the top of your cupcakes, cut out 12 circles and place them carefully on top of the jam.

Make the fondant icing and pour on top of the marzipan. Leave to dry thoroughly.

Lightly dust a work surface with cornflour (cornstarch) and roll out the sugar paste (rolled fondant) until it is about 3 mm/⅛in thick. Cut out 12 large stars and 12 smaller stars.

When the fondant is dry, put a tiny dab of edible glue on the centre of each cake and place a large star on top. Then put a dab of glue on the centre of the star and place the smaller star on top.

With a cocktail stick (toothpick) make a little indent in the centre of the top star and, again with the cocktail stick, apply a smidgen of edible glue. Carefully put one silver dragee into this little indent.

# Index

# Acknowledgements

There are several cake people that I would really like to thank for being great inspirations and incredibly generous with their knowledge and skills in their own books. Peggy Porschen and Annie Bell have both been hugely important culinary companions in a literary sense. I'd also like to thank Nigella Lawson for really putting cupcakes on the map! If you don't have *How to Be a Domestic Goddess: Baking and the Art of Comfort Cooking*, get it. It's a really good book.

Thanks to The Orange Tree in Exeter for lending me all sorts of lovely accoutrements. Thank you, Charlotte Barton, for the gorgeous photos and always seeming to have the perfect cup, tablecloth or cake stand to hand at just the right moment – and for telling me when my ideas were rubbish.

My delightful models, Tom, Emma and Rory, deserve a special mention for eating large quantities of cake on demand and never failing to remain cheerful and lacking in vomity-type behaviour. The hens did well, too. Thanks, girls.

Thanks, Emily, at Pavilion, for being a very positive person and not remotely flappy.

Finally, thank you to Tarek and the rest of my family and friends, for tolerating this obsession with good humour and constant words of encouragement.